dBASE IV

A Tutorial to Accompany
Peter Norton's Introduction to Computers

Miguel Pendás

GLENCOE
Macmillan/McGraw-Hill

New York, New York • Columbus, Ohio • Mission Hills, California • Peoria, Illinois

Library of Congress Cataloging-in-Publication Data

Pendás, Miguel.
    dBASE IV: A Tutorial to Accompany Peter Norton's Introduction to
Computers / Miguel Pendás.
      p.   cm.
    Includes index.
    ISBN 0-02-801327-1
    1. Database management.   2. dBASE IV (Computer file)
I. Norton, Peter, 1943– Introduction to computers. II. Title.
    QA76.9.D3P444   1994   93-23741
    005.75'65—dc20   CIP

Concept, Development, and Production: BMR, Corte Madera, Ca.

dBASE IV: A Tutorial to Accompany Peter Norton's Introduction to Computers

Send all inquiries to:

GLENCOE DIVISION
Macmillan/McGraw-Hill
936 Eastwind Drive
Westerville, OH 43081

ISBN 0-02-801327-1

 2 3 4 5 6 7 8 9 BANT 99 98 97 96 95 94

dBASE IV is a registered trademark of Borland International
WordPerfect is a registered trademark of WordPerfect Corporation.
Lotus and 1-2-3 are registered trademarks of Lotus Development Corporation.
MS-DOS is a registered trademark of WordPerfect Corporation.
MS-Windows is a trademark of Microsoft Corporation.

CONTENTS

PREFACE

Almost everything we do in our information society depends to some extent on information technology. Because the way we manage information has become increasingly sophisticated, the need for strong conceptual computer skills has increased. This book will help readers become intelligent users of the forward-looking technology that is incorporated in dBASE IV.

This *dBASE IV Tutorial* is only one of the instructional tools that complement *Peter Norton's Introduction to Computers*. Glencoe and Peter Norton have teamed up to provide a new approach to computer education, one not reflected in traditional computer textbooks. The text and its ancillary materials are grounded in the philosophy that it is knowledgeable end users who will provide the gains in productivity that both businesses and individuals need to achieve in the 1990s and beyond. Mere button pushing is not enough; in order to handle more and more complex computer tasks, both in the workplace and in the home, computer users must understand the concepts behind their computer hardware and software.

Database Work Advances into the Future

Database software has evolved dramatically since the first database management programs were created. Today's database programs allow users to take advantage of a vast array of features, including menu-driven interfaces and tools like dBASE's Application Generator, which lets users create applications by manipulating objects rather than by writing code. Today's database software allows users to do much more than structure and manipulate information. By making use of such advanced features as graphics, users can create complex documents on their personal computers, something that just a few years ago could have been done only by programmers or other computer specialists.

Structure and Format of the dBASE IV Tutorial

The purpose of this tutorial is to help students apply some of the important concepts covered in *Peter Norton's Introduction to Computers*. The value of the tutorial is increased if users have a good understanding of the concepts covered in the text. However, students can use the tutorial even as they take their first steps toward understanding computers.

In each of the three lessons contained in the *dBASE IV Tutorial*, students work their way through several step-by-step exercises. They progress at their own pace, repeating difficult sections as necessary. Although it is assumed that students will be working with a mouse, keyboard alternatives are included in the Command Summary near the end of each lesson. Each lesson concludes with review questions as well as hands-on applications of the techniques covered in the lesson. A glossary at the end of the book makes it easy for students to review key terms and refresh their memories.

Other Instructional Support

To provide instructors with additional resources for administering their courses, Glencoe has developed an innovative *Instructor's Productivity Center (IPC)*. The *IPC* contains not only the computerized testbank , but also selected files from the *Instructor's Manual and Key,* electronic transparencies, Peter Norton newsletter updates, and student data files that correspond to the innovative "Exploring Your Computer" section—hands-on exercises at the end of the main text.

The *dBASE IV Tutorial* also has its own *Instructor's Manual and Key,* with hints and teaching tips, lecture outlines, answers to end-of-lesson questions, and additional application projects.

Almost everything we do, whether at home or in the workplace, can be done better if we increase our understanding of the tools we use. We hope this tutorial, and all the components of the *Peter Norton's Introduction to Computers* package, allows students to make intelligent choices about the way they use computers in their personal and professional lives.

Figure 1-8

Write a description for a catalog to help you remember what it is used for.

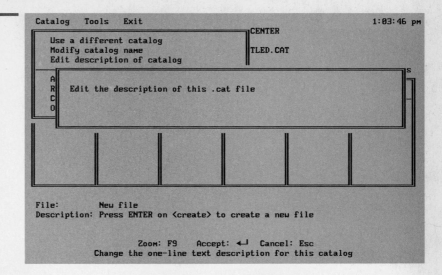

14. Press (Esc).

    The Catalog menu closes.

Another way of opening a menu besides pressing (F10) is to press (Alt) and the first letter of the name of the menu.

15. Press (Alt)-T.

    The Tools menu opens, as shown in Figure 1-10. The arrow next to certain menu items means that choosing that item leads to another menu. The cursor is on Macros.

16. Press (↓) to move the cursor to Import.

17. Press (Enter).

    The Import menu appears. In this menu, you can import files from other applications.

18. Press (Esc).

19. Press (↓) twice to move the cursor to DOS Utilities.

Figure 1-9

When you choose Add File to Catalog, a file choice list box appears.

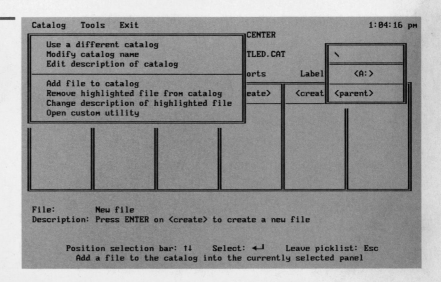

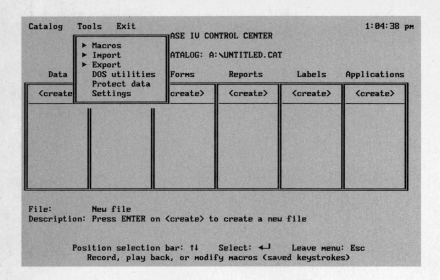

Figure 1-10

The Tools menu. The arrow next to certain entries means that choosing this command leads to another menu.

20. Press [Enter].

The DOS Utilities screen appears, as shown in Figure 1-11. Here you can carry out DOS operations such as creating directories and moving files. In the center is a directory that reflects the file directory in DOS. At the top of this screen is a menu bar.

21. Press [F10].

The DOS pop-up menu opens with three choices, as shown in Figure 1-12.

22. Press [↓] to choose Go to DOS.

23. Press [Enter].

You are now at the DOS command line, even though dBASE IV is still running. Here you can issue a DOS command.

24. Type **exit** and press [Enter].

You return to the DOS Utilities screen.

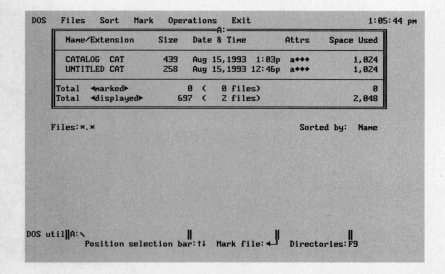

Figure 1-11

You can carry out DOS commands and browse directories at the DOS Utilities screen.

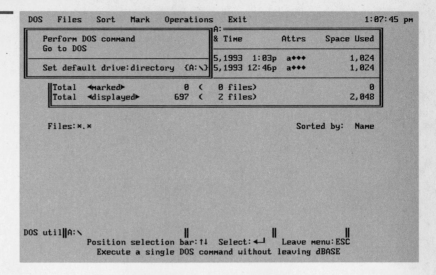

Figure 1-12

The DOS **pop-up menu** lets you perform DOS commands.

25. Press Alt-D, move the cursor to Set Default Drive: Directory, and press Enter.

*A **fill-in box** appears, as in Figure 1-13. Here you type the path name of the directory and drive you want to be in. (If you forget to start dBASE from drive A and end up lost, this is a handy command to remember. Type **A:** and press Enter here to change to drive A.)*

26. Press Esc.

The fill-in box closes.

27. Press Alt-E, Enter.

You return to the Control Center.

The Panels

This is the area where you create, modify, open, and close files. The panels list the different kinds of files in the current catalog. When the Control Center first opens, the cursor is by default on <create> in the Data panel. This panel lists all data files, that is, those

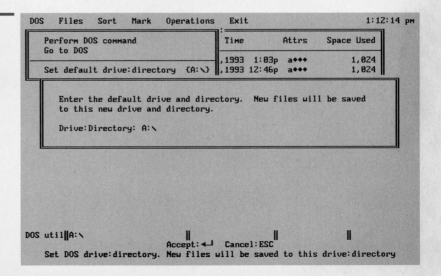

Figure 1-13

Choose Set Default Drive: Directory to change the drive or directory you are currently in.

with a .DBF extension. A **data file** is, in effect, a database, and we will use the terms interchangeably. In the example used earlier of the customer list for the copier supply company, this type of file would contain the customer data that are organized into fields and records.

To use an existing data file, you move the cursor down to a file name below the line in the Data panel and press [Enter]. dBASE opens the file and places the name above the line. Only one data file can be open at a time. To open a new data file, press [Enter] with the cursor on <create> in the Data panel. This will lead you to the database design screen, as shown in Figure 1-14. This is where you define the fields for a database: the field name, the field type, the width, and so on.

A **field name** is limited to ten characters and can include the letters of the alphabet, numerals, and the underscore character (_), but no empty spaces. There are two main **field types: character** and **numeric**. A character field can contain numerals, but the numbers will be treated as text, not as quantities on which you can perform arithmetical calculations. For example, a field that contains a street address or a social security number should be a character field, even though it has numbers in it. You would not want to perform calculations with "123 Main Street" or "266-70-9770." You would probably define fields, however, that contained employee salaries, number of deductions, and tax rates as numeric, so that you could calculate an employee's weekly paycheck.

dBASE provides a **date field** that automatically formats a date into month, day, and year and is limited to eight spaces (MM/DD/YY). You can change this to conform to styles of writing the date in countries such as Japan (YY/MM/DD) or Europe and Latin America (DD/MM/YY).

Another field type is **logical**, which can accept only yes/no (**Y** or **N**) or true/false (**T** or **F**) as an entry. A **memo field** allows you to create a note.

After you define each characteristic for the first field, press [Enter] and continue for as many other fields as you wish to have. Even after you define the fields and enter data, you can still come back to this screen to make modifications in the structure.

```
Layout   Organize   Append   Go To   Exit                    1:13:17 pm
                                          Bytes remaining:    4000
┌─────┬────────────┬────────────┬───────┬─────┬───────┐
│ Num │ Field Name │ Field Type │ Width │ Dec │ Index │
├─────┼────────────┼────────────┼───────┼─────┼───────┤
│  1  │            │ Character  │       │     │   N   │
│     │            │            │       │     │       │
│     │            │            │       │     │       │
│     │            │            │       │     │       │
│     │            │            │       │     │       │
│     │            │            │       │     │       │
│     │            │            │       │     │       │
│     │            │            │       │     │       │
│     │            │            │       │     │       │
└─────┴────────────┴────────────┴───────┴─────┴───────┘
Database║A:\<NEW>              ║Field 1/1    ║         ║
         Enter the field name.  Insert/Delete field:Ctrl-N/Ctrl-U
Field names begin with a letter and may contain letters, digits and underscores
```

Figure 1-14

At the database design screen, you decide how many fields your data file will have and of what type.

Figure 1-15

At the query design screen, you ask dBASE questions in order to obtain information.

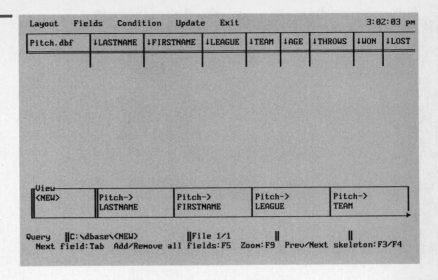

Queries

Another kind of file is the **query,** which you create at the **query design screen** shown in Figure 1-15. You query a database when you want to know the answer to specific questions such as "Which of my customers spend more than $500 a month on copier supplies?" Assuming you had the foresight to include a field in your database that shows monthly sales figures for each customer, a query will answer that question quickly, even if your database contains thousands of entries.

Forms

dBASE has a **default data entry form**, also known as the **Edit screen**, which is based on the fields of the database. Figure 1-16 is an example. In this standard entry form, the fields are in order of field number, and they are labeled with the name of the field. The number of spaces available for data entry corresponds to the width of the field as you defined it.

Figure 1-16

You can use the Edit screen as a default data entry form.

15. Press (Pg Dn).

dBASE asks if you want to add new records.

16. Press Y.

A new blank record appears.

17. Enter the data below in the appropriate fields to create the next three records, as in steps 5-13.

Palladio, Scamozzi & Bernini, 157 Church St, Venice, CA, 90655; 311-601-7755 (Andy)

Gropius Design, 7811 N Cambridge Ave, Los Angeles, CA, 90817; 211-925-3169 (Walt)

Latrobe, Thornton & Bulfinch, 400 Bank St, Philadelphia, PA, 70196; 724-932-8041 (Ben)

18. Press (Esc).

You return to the Control Center.

Displaying Data

Another way to display data is the **Browse screen**, shown in Figure 1-30. As you can see, all the fields are shown in columns and rows like a table. Like the Edit screen, the Browse screen is just another way of looking at your data file; however, it cannot be used until there are some records in the file. You toggle between the two by pressing (F2). The Browse screen shows all the records, in natural order. Each column represents a field, and each row represents a record. You can also add and change records at this screen, but most people consider it more convenient for viewing the file as a whole than for data entry. For one thing, a record in a database with many fields may stretch out beyond the right edge of the Browse screen.

At the top of the Browse and Edit screens is the menu bar. To use the menus, press (F10), as you do in the Control Center when you want to use a menu. You can also press (Alt) plus the first letter of the menu you want.

Figure 1.30

The Browse screen displays all the records at once; it can also be used for data entry.

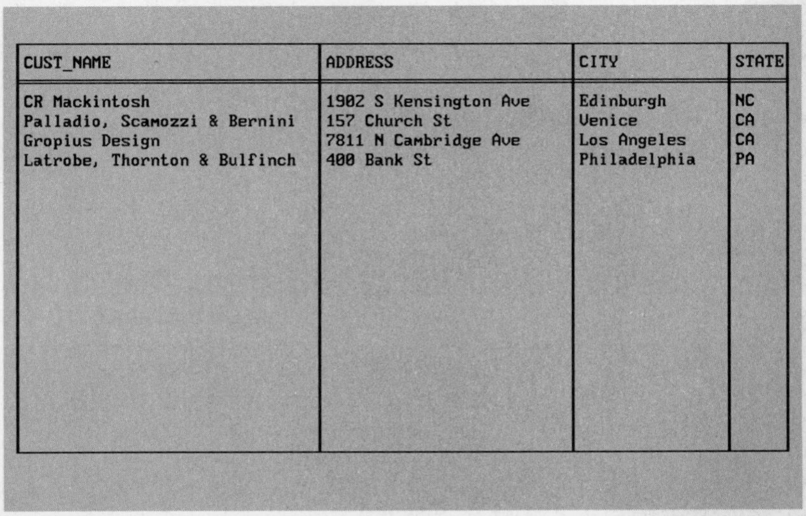

CUST_NAME	ADDRESS	CITY	STATE
CR Mackintosh	1902 S Kensington Ave	Edinburgh	NC
Palladio, Scamozzi & Bernini	157 Church St	Venice	CA
Gropius Design	7811 N Cambridge Ave	Los Angeles	CA
Latrobe, Thornton & Bulfinch	400 Bank St	Philadelphia	PA

The status bar near the bottom of the screen tells you the directory and path name of the data file you are in, the number of the record, and the total number of records. For example, Rec 4/17 means you are in record 4 out of a total of 17 records.

You can change the display of data to some extent to make it easier to see. For example, if you are working in a data file that has a lot of fields, they may not all fit on the Browse screen. If you are working in the CUSTOMRS file, by the time you move the cursor to the last fields on the right, you cannot see the name of the customer in the first field. This could lead to confusion and mistakes in data entry. There are a couple of things you can do.

You can use Tab and Shift-Tab to move back and forth across the columns. Another approach is to lock the first field in place so that it always remains on screen even when you scroll to the right. To do this, choose Lock Fields on Left from the Fields menu, shown in Figure 1-31. A dialog box appears, asking you how many fields you want to remain stationary. Specify the number and press Enter. Now those fields are locked until you change the number back to zero.

If you don't need to see the entire contents of each field, you can "squeeze" one or more fields for display purposes. To resize a field, place the cursor in the field you want to squeeze and choose Size Field from the Fields menu. You will be prompted to use the arrow keys to narrow or widen the field.

Another handy command in the Fields menu of the Browse screen is the Freeze Field command. When you want to work in only one field of a data file, this command restricts cursor movement to the field number you specify, thus saving you a lot of unnecessary cursor movement. To unfreeze the cursor, press the same command and erase the field name.

Quick Reports

Sometimes you want to see a hard copy of a database, without going to the trouble of creating a full-fledged report. You can do this easily with the Quick Reports command, from the Control Center. **Quick reports** give you the basics: all the data arranged in

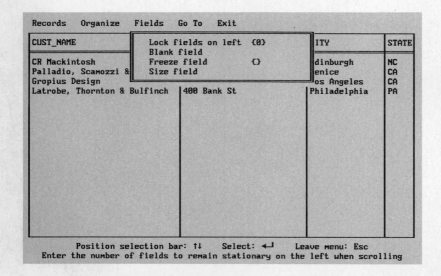

Figure 1-31

You can choose to lock fields in place to keep them in view.

rows and columns, with the name of each field at the top of each column, and the date and page number on each page.

To generate a quick report, you must first be in the Control Center. In the Data panel, highlight the name of the data file you want. Press [Shift]-[F9] (the navigation line reminds you that this is the command for a quick report). A print menu appears, as shown in Figure 1-32. You can just highlight Begin Printing and press [Enter], and the file prints.

One drawback with quick reports is that if each record is longer than the page is wide, the line breaks, and this makes it a bit confusing to read. If your printer is capable of printing condensed type, you can use the Print menu to select this option and allow an entire record to fit lengthwise in many cases. To do this, highlight Control of Printer in the Print menu and press [Enter]. The menu in Figure 1-33 appears. With the cursor on Text Pitch, press [Spacebar] until the word "CONDENSED" comes up. Press [Esc] to close this menu and then print.

Use the Browse Screen to Print a Quick Report

Now you will use the Browse screen to enter a few more records into the CUSTOMRS database and then print a quick report. Make sure you are working in drive A, your work disk is in drive A, and the cursor is at the Control Center. The catalog bar should read A:\PRACTICE.CAT. The name of the data file you created, CUSTOMRS, is listed in the Data panel.

1. Press [↓] to highlight CUSTOMRS.

2. Press [Enter].

   The dialog box appears.

3. Press [→] twice to highlight Display Data.

4. Press [Enter].

   Either the Edit screen or the Browse screen appears, depending on which you displayed last.

Figure 1-32

Press [Shift]-[F9] to see the print menu for a quick report.

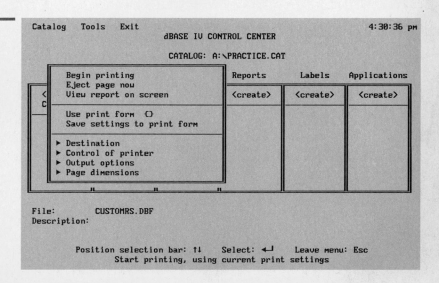

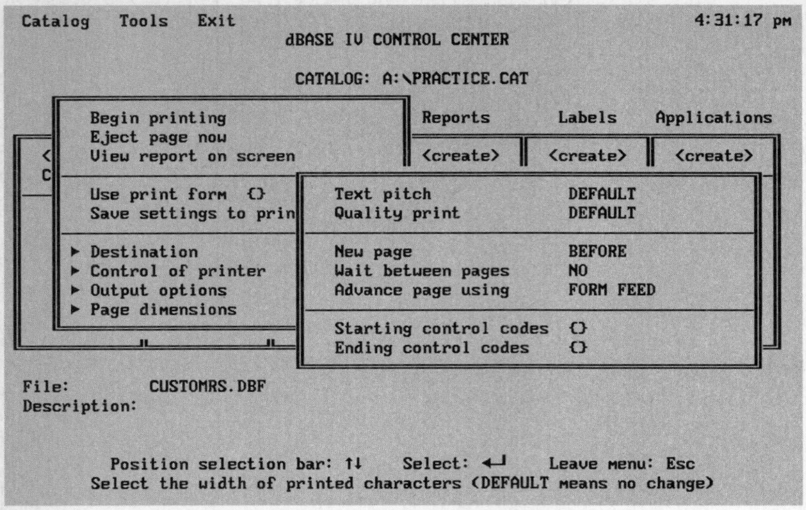

```
Catalog  Tools  Exit                                    4:31:17 PM
                        dBASE IV CONTROL CENTER
                        CATALOG: A:\PRACTICE.CAT
  ┌──────────────────────────┬──────────────────────────────────────┐
  │  Begin printing          │   Reports      Labels   Applications  │
  │  Eject page now          │                                       │
 <│  View report on screen   │  <create>    <create>    <create>     │
 C│                          ├──────────────────────────┐            │
  │  Use print form  {}      │  Text pitch       DEFAULT │           │
  │  Save settings to prin│  │  Quality print    DEFAULT │           │
  │                          │                           │           │
  │ ► Destination            │  New page         BEFORE  │           │
  │ ► Control of printer     │  Wait between pages    NO │           │
  │ ► Output options         │  Advance page using FORM FEED │       │
  │ ► Page dimensions        │                           │           │
  │                          │  Starting control codes {}│           │
  └──────┴────────────┴──────┤  Ending control codes   {}│           │
                             └───────────────────────────┘
File:       CUSTOMRS.DBF
Description:


        Position selection bar: ↑↓     Select: ↵      Leave menu: Esc
        Select the width of printed characters (DEFAULT means no change)
```

Figure 1-33

Choosing Control of Printer leads to another menu, where you can choose more printing options, such as condensing text pitch to squeeze more information on the page.

5. If you are in the Edit screen, press F2 to change to the Browse screen.

The Browse screen appears, as in Figure 1-34, showing the previous four records you entered.

6. Press ↓ until you are prompted as to whether to add a new record, and type **Y**.

7. Enter the next four records at the Browse screen, using the data below (be sure to put the data in the right field):

Tatlin Construction, 1300 Academy Blvd, Moscow, ID, 19902; 533-921-5771 (Vlade)

Saarinen & Son, 611 Fifth Ave, Suite 570, New York, NY, 10016; 232-209-1014 (Judy)

Sullivan & Adler, 1884 W Ryerson St, Chicago, IL, 60874; 332-781-4811 (Adrienne)

Salvi Fountain Specialties, 1732 Neptune St, Rome, NY, 11751; 337-971-1596 (Nick)

So far you have entered eight records into your database. It should now look like Figure 1-35.

8. Press Esc.

You return to the Control Center. Next you will do a quick report.

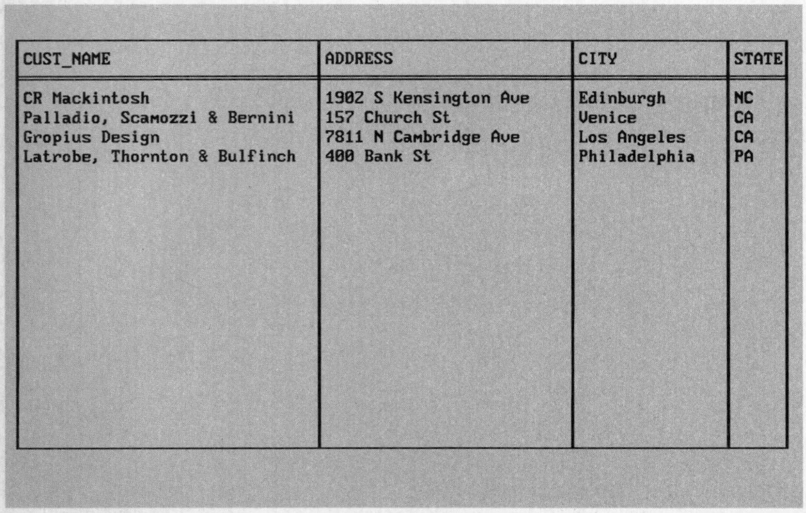

CUST_NAME	ADDRESS	CITY	STATE
CR Mackintosh	1902 S Kensington Ave	Edinburgh	NC
Palladio, Scamozzi & Bernini	157 Church St	Venice	CA
Gropius Design	7811 N Cambridge Ave	Los Angeles	CA
Latrobe, Thornton & Bulfinch	400 Bank St	Philadelphia	PA

Figure 1-34

The Browse screen displays the records you created in the previous exercise.

9. Press Shift - F9.

The Print menu appears. Be sure your printer is turned on.

10. With Begin Printing highlighted, press Enter.

The quick report of your data file prints. Note that each record wraps to a second line because it is too long to fit on one line. Depending on your printer, the whole line may not print.

Designing an Entry Form

To make data entry as easy, efficient, and accurate as possible, dBASE gives you the option of designing **custom data entry forms**.

The standard entry form of the Edit screen is convenient, but it may not always be the ideal format for data entry. For one thing, field names are sometimes abbreviated, and the person who actually enters the data may not know what a field name stands for. Also, data is frequently entered into a computer from paper forms that are arranged quite differently from the way you defined the fields in the database. You may find it more convenient, for data entry purposes, to create a custom data entry form in which you have the freedom to arrange the fields in a different order, put several fields on one line, or label them differently. Some extra spaces, lines, and boxes may also make things easier for the eye to follow. You can do all this by creating a custom entry form at the **form design screen**.

To design a custom entry form, begin by opening the data file you want to create the form for. Then move the cursor over to the Forms panel to highlight <create>, and press Enter to open the form design screen, shown in Figure 1-36.

The ruler across the top of the work space helps you to line things up. There are ten columns (ten spaces) to an inch, and each inch is marked with a number. Column 20 appears two inches (20 spaces) from the left, for example, under the number 2. Column 23 appears three spaces to the right of that, and so on.

Figure 1-35

The browse screen now shows the additional screens that you added.

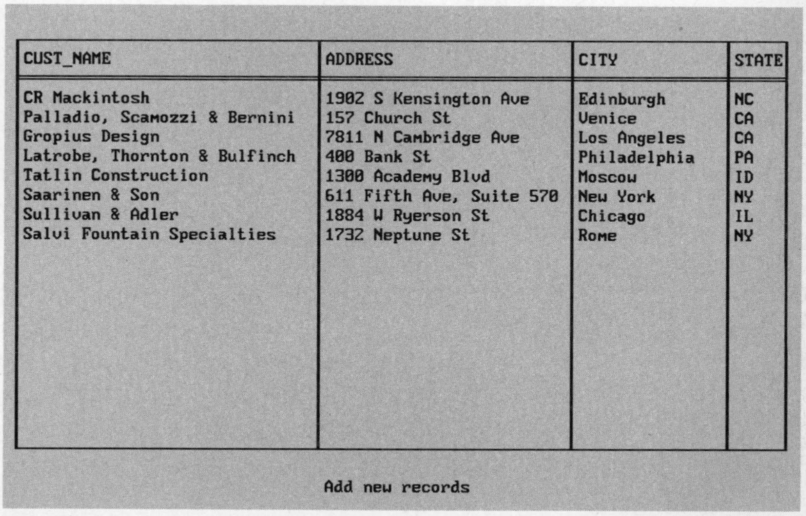

CUST_NAME	ADDRESS	CITY	STATE
CR Mackintosh	1902 S Kensington Ave	Edinburgh	NC
Palladio, Scamozzi & Bernini	157 Church St	Venice	CA
Gropius Design	7811 N Cambridge Ave	Los Angeles	CA
Latrobe, Thornton & Bulfinch	400 Bank St	Philadelphia	PA
Tatlin Construction	1300 Academy Blvd	Moscow	ID
Saarinen & Son	611 Fifth Ave, Suite 570	New York	NY
Sullivan & Adler	1884 W Ryerson St	Chicago	IL
Salvi Fountain Specialties	1732 Neptune St	Rome	NY

Add new records

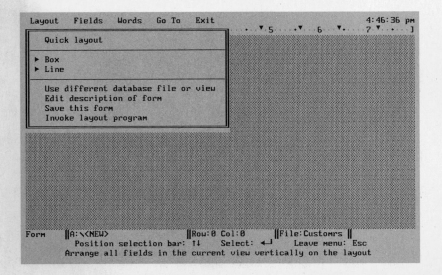

```
 Layout   Fields   Words   Go To   Exit                    4:45:37 pm
[ · · · · ▼ · 1 · · · ▼ · · · 2 · · · ▼ · · · 3 ▼ · · · · · · ▼ · 5 · · · · ▼ · · 6 · · ▼ · · · 7 ▼ · · · · 1




 Form    ‖A:\<NEW>            ‖Row:0 Col:0    ‖File:Customrs ‖           Ins
              Add field:F5  Select:F6  Move:F7  Copy:F8  Size:Shift-F7
```

Figure 1-36

The ruler at the top of the form design screen helps you to keep things lined up when you design a custom entry form.

Next you add the fields to the form. One way to do this is to open the Layout menu, shown in Figure 1-37, and to use the Quick Layout command, which puts all the fields on the form at once, in the same arrangement as the Edit screen. You can then use [F7] (Move) and [Shift]-[F7] (Size) to move things around to suit yourself.

If you plan to change things around a lot, though, it may actually be faster to add the fields to the form one at a time. First, place the cursor where you want the field to appear. Then, choose Add Field under the Fields menu, or just use the shortcut, [F5]. A list box with all the fields appears. Highlight the one you want and press [Enter], and the field appears on the work surface of the form design screen, in the spot where you placed the cursor. A note of caution: Never place a field in the top row of the form design screen. When you go to use the entry form, that row will be covered by the menu bar.

Unlike the data in a data file that is automatically saved as you work, a design is not saved until you save it. It's not a bad idea to save your form each time you have a field placed to your satisfaction. To save, choose Save This Form from the Layout menu. When you are prompted to name the form, use a name that conforms to DOS standards, that is, any combination of eight letters, numerals, dash, or underscore.

```
 Layout   Fields   Words   Go To   Exit                    4:46:36 pm
┌────────────────────────────────────┐ · · · ▼ · 5 · · · · ▼ · · · ▼ · · · 6 · · ▼ · · · 7 ▼ · · · · 1
│   Quick layout                      │
│                                     │
│ ► Box                               │
│ ► Line                              │
│                                     │
│   Use different database file or view│
│   Edit description of form          │
│   Save this form                    │
│   Invoke layout program             │
└────────────────────────────────────┘


 Form    ‖A:\<NEW>            ‖Row:0 Col:0    ‖File:Customrs ‖
              Position selection bar: ↑↓   Select: ↵   Leave menu: Esc
          Arrange all fields in the current view vertically on the layout
```

Figure 1-37

The layout menu on the form design screen lets you put all the fields on the screen at once with the Quick Layout command.

To move a field after you place it on the screen, you must first select it. Place the cursor in the field, press F6 (Select), and then press Enter to complete the selection. If you want to select several fields, place the cursor at the beginning of the first field you want to select and press F6 . Move the cursor with the arrow keys until the highlighting covers all the fields you want, then press Enter to complete the selection. The whole area will be highlighted as in Figure 1-38.

After you select what you want to move, press F7 (Move). Then press the arrow keys and watch the selection move on the screen. When you arrive at the desired new location, press Enter to complete the operation.

If you move the selection on top of something else on the screen and press Enter, dBASE advises you that if you complete the move, you will wipe out whatever is underneath. If you choose Yes, the placement is completed; if you choose No, the operation is canceled.

When dBASE first places a field on the work surface of the form design screen, the name of the field also appears next to it. You can delete or change this text. For example, if you have a field with a cryptic name like CUST_NAME, you may want to change the label to something like Customer Name so that other people can figure out what it's for. You might also want to add a title or instructions to the form. You can add or change text anywhere on the design screen that is not a data field. Just place the cursor where you want and start typing. It is not unlike typing text with a word processing program in Type-over mode.

To create an extra line, choose Add Line from the Words menu. Or, toggle into insert mode by pressing Ins and then Enter. To center text, or to place it flush right or flush left, choose Position from the Words menu and then choose Center, Right, or Left.

Design a Custom Entry Form

Now you will design a custom entry form for the CUSTOMRS database that looks like the entry form in Figure 1-39. Make sure you are working in drive A, your work disk is in drive A, and the cursor is at the Control Center.

Figure 1-38

Use the F6 (Select) command to highlight fields or text that you want to move.

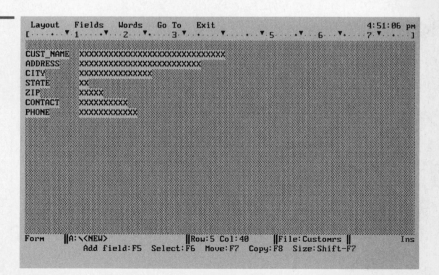

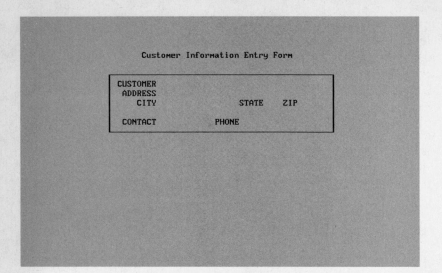

Figure 1-39

You will design a data entry form that looks like this.

1. Move the cursor to CUSTOMRS in the Data panel and press [Enter].

   The dialog box opens.

2. Press [Enter] to choose Use File.

3. Press [→] to move the cursor to the Forms panel.

4. Press [Enter] to choose <create>.

   The form design screen appears, with the cursor in the upper left corner of the workspace. First, you will use the Quick Layout command to enter the fields.

5. Press [Alt]-L.

   The Layout menu opens (if it isn't open already).

6. Highlight Quick Layout and press [Enter].

   All the fields are on the workspace now, as in Figure 1-40. This would be a good time to save your work.

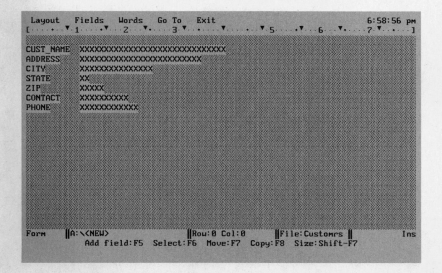

Figure 1-40

The Quick Layout command copies the fields to the form.

7. Press [Alt]-L to open the Layout menu and choose Save This Form.

dBASE prompts you for a name for the file.

8. Type **a:custform** and press [Enter].

dBASE saves the entry form as A:CUSTFORM.SCR. Now you will begin to arrange the fields.

9. Press [Ins] to turn on Insert mode.

The letters "Ins" appear in the status bar near the bottom of the screen.

10. Press [Enter] five times.

The fields and text move down five lines. Next you will type the title.

11. Press [↑] twice and [→] to move to column 24. (The status bar tells you which row and column the cursor is in.)

You should be at row 3, column 24.

12. Type **Customer Information Entry Form**.

13. Use the arrow keys to move the cursor to the first X in the CUST_NAME field, which should be row 6, column 11.

As soon as the cursor enters the field, the field becomes highlighted, as in Figure 1-41.

14. Press [F6] (Select) and then [Enter] to complete the selection.

15. Press [F7] (Move).

16. Move the cursor to column 28 and then press [Enter] to complete the move.

A dialog box appears, shown in Figure 1-42, asking if you want to delete what's underneath the cursor.

17. Press Y to indicate Yes.

The field moves to the new spot.

Figure 1-41

As soon as the cursor enters any part of a field, the entire field is highlighted.

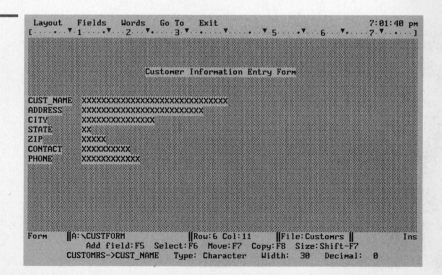

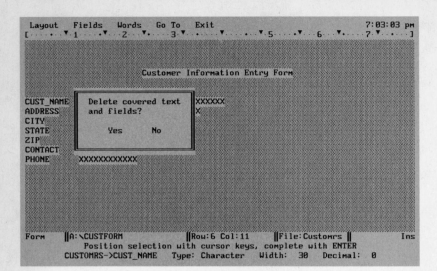

Figure 1-42

If you use F7 (Move) to move something over existing text or fields, dBASE warns you that the covered material will be deleted.

18. Repeat steps 13-17 to move the ADDRESS and CITY fields to column 28.

19. Move the cursor to column 44, leaving one blank space after the end of the CITY field.

20. Type **STATE**

21. Move the cursor to the STATE field, press F6 (Select), and press Enter.

22. Press F7 (Move).

23. Move the cursor to row 8, column 50, leaving one blank space after the word STATE.

24. Press Enter to complete the move.

    The screen should now look like Figure 1-43.

25. Move the cursor past the STATE field, to row 8, column 53, leaving one blank space.

26. Type **ZIP**

27. Move the ZIP field after the word ZIP, leaving a space.

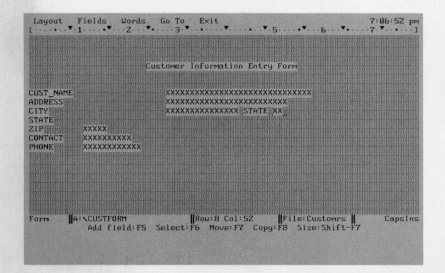

Figure 1-43

You move the fields around using F6 (Select) and F7 (Move).

28. Move the CONTACT field to row 10, column 28, leaving a blank row after the CITY field.

29. Type **PHONE** after the CONTACT field and move the PHONE field after the new name.

Your screen should now look like Figure 1-44. If not, use the Select and Move commands to fix it up. The only thing left to do is type in a few more field names and put a box around the whole thing.

30. Move the cursor to column 19 of row 6, the row with the CUST_NAME field, and type **CUSTOMER**

31. Type the other field names **ADDRESS**, **CITY**, and **CONTACT** so that they are lined up as in Figure 1-30.

32. Using the arrow keys, (Bksp), and (Del), erase all the old field names.

33. Move the cursor to row 5, column 17 of the row above the CUSTOMER field.

34. Press (Alt)-L and choose Box.

A list box appears, allowing you to choose from a selection of boxes and lines.

35. Highlight Single Line and press (Enter) twice.

36. Move the cursor down to row 11, one row past the CONTACT field, and to the right one space past the last character of the ZIP field, to column 63.

37. Press (Enter).

The box appears. Your entry form is complete. It should look like Figure 1-45. Make any cosmetic changes necessary so that your form looks like the example. After making final changes, you are ready to save and exit the design screen.

39. Press (Alt)-E.

40. Choose Save Changes and Exit.

You return to the Control Center, where CUSTFORM is now displayed in the Forms panel.

Figure 1-44

After you have moved the fields where you want them, retype the labels.

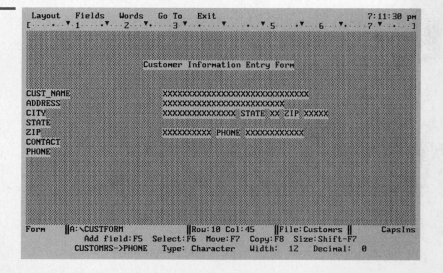

3. Create a database to keep track of the architectural supply company's inventory.

    a. Create data file A:STOCK.

    b. The file should have seven fields with the following characteristics:

Field Name	Type	Width	Dec	Index
PART_NO	Character	15		Y
DESCRIPTN	Character	25		N
COST	Numeric	8	2	N
PRICE	Numeric	8	2	N
ON_HAND	Numeric	5	0	N
REORD_AT	Numeric	5	0	N
AUTO_REORD	Logical	1		N

    c. Enter the following parts into the database.

description	Part#	On Hand	Cost	Price	Reorder At	Auto Reorder
arch	10001	13	200.00	400.00	10	N
corbel	10002	34	35.00	70.00	25	Y
lintel	10003	7	135.00	270.00	8	N
capital, Doric	10004	16	325.00	650.00	10	N
capital, Ionic	10005	42	375.00	750.00	20	N
capital, Corinthian	10006	66	450.00	900.00	30	N
balustrade	10007	228	16.75	33.50	75	Y
joist	10008	320	8.33	16.50	120	Y
beam	10009	183	9.07	18.25	80	Y
pilaster	10010	55	205.00	410.00	15	N
column	10011	178	420.75	845.00	90	Y
bead	10012	479	4.12	8.25	150	Y
rail	10013	145	12.33	24.75	75	Y
base	10014	188	9.39	18.90	150	Y
drawer pull	10015	0	4.19	8.40	25	N

4. In this exercise you will make some changes to the files you created in Lesson 1.

    a. Change the entry form CUSTFORM for the CUSTOMRS database to reflect the two new fields you added (CREDIT_LMT and PREFERRED) in the exercise "Modifying a Database Structure."

b. Add a field to the STOCK database to list the wholesale source for the company's inventory parts, with the following attributes:

Field Name	Type	Width	Dec	Index
SOURCE	Character	25		Y

c. Then, fill in the field in each record for part numbers 0001 through 0015.

Part No.	Supplier
0001	Bloch, Stone & Wood
0002	Acme Details
0003	Exteriors
0004	Bloch, Stone & Wood
0005	Bloch, Stone & Wood
0006	Bloch, Stone & Wood
0007	Elements, Inc.
0008	Ren & Riser Suppliers
0009	Ren & Riser Suppliers
0010	Exteriors
0011	Elements, Inc
0012	Acme Details
0013	Arnold's Hardware
0014	Elements, Inc
0015	Arnold's Hardware

LESSON 2   MAINTAINING DATABASE RECORDS

Objectives

After completing this lesson, you will be able to do the following:

- Calculate database data.
- Edit existing records in a data file.
- Search for a record.
- Delete records.
- Sort records.
- Create an index.
- Generate reports.
- Query a database.

Changing Records

Editing a record involves little more than what adding new records did. The main difference is that you first have to locate the record that you want to change. In small databases, such as the ones you have created in the exercises in this book, finding a record is not a problem, since you can usually see them all on one Browse screen. If you display the Edit screen, you can press Pg Up or Pg Dn to move up and down through the records in natural order. In a more typical situation, however, there will be thousands of records, and to find a particular one you will have to use dBASE **search** commands.

Let's say that you want to find the contact person's name for a company in the CUS-TOMRS database, Gropius Design. dBASE will search the data in a particular field for all the records until it finds the character string that you specified. To use the search command, you must be in either the Edit screen or the Browse screen. To find Gropius Design, first place the cursor in the customer name field of any record. Then press F10 to display the menu and select the Go To menu, shown in Figure 2-1. Then select Forward Search. A fill-in box prompts you for the character string you are looking for. You type **Gropius Design** and press Enter. Before you know it, dBASE moves the record pointer to that record.

That was easy because you knew the exact name of the company. dBASE looks for an exact match. But what if you couldn't remember the exact name or didn't spell it right? That's where wild-card characters come in handy. You can use the asterisk (*) as a wild card, just as in DOS commands. A **wild card** is a character that substitutes for any other character or sequence of characters. For example, if all you can remember about a company is that Scamozzi is part of the name, you could search for *Scamozzi*, and dBASE would find Palladio, Scamozzi & Bernini.

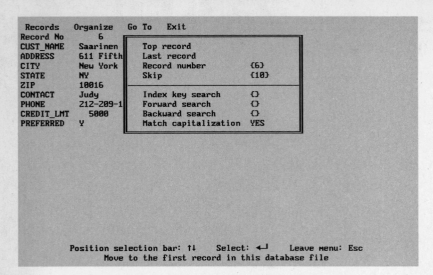

Figure 2-1

You can conduct a search for a record with the Go To menu.

Of course, using the wild card means that there may be more than one record that fits the description. If you search for the string "*Design," there may be several companies that fit that description. In that case, dBASE will find the first one; then you issue the command again, and dBASE will find the next one; and so on, until you find what you want.

It's a good idea to begin a search from the top of the database; otherwise, you will search only from the present location. To go to the top, choose Top from the the Go To menu. If you know the exact number of the record you want, you can specify that number with the Go To Record command in the Go To menu.

Once you've found the record you want, making changes is a simple matter of placing the cursor in the field you want to change and typing in the changes. You use the [Del] and [Bksp] keys as you normally would. Don't forget that dBASE is normally in Typeover mode, so if you want to insert characters into a field without typing over what's already there, press [Ins] to change to Insert mode.

If you are changing a record and make a mistake, you can undo the changes with the Undo Change to Record command in the Record menu, shown in Figure 2-2. However,

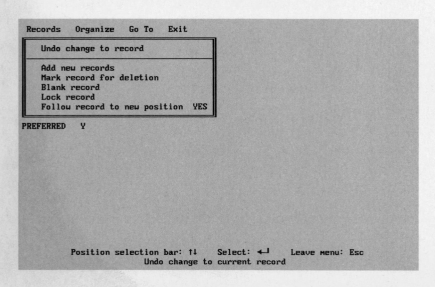

Figure 2-2

The Undo Change to Record command will undo any changes you have made in a record before you move the cursor to another record.

dBASE automatically saves the changes as soon as you move to another record, and then you cannot undo the changes with the undo command.

Search for Records and Make Changes

Now you will use search commands to find records in the CUSTOMRS database, make changes, and save them. Make sure you are working in drive A, your work disk is in drive A, and the cursor is at the Control Center.

1. Activate the CUSTFORM data entry screen.

2. Press F2.

The Edit screen appears as shown in Figure 2-3. You have been told that the Barragan company has a new street address, and now you must update your files. First, search for the Barragan record.

3. With the cursor in the CUSTOMER field, press F10.

The menu bar appears.

4. Press → until the Go To menu opens.

5. Press ↓ to highlight Forward Search and press Enter.

The fill-in box asking you for a search string appears, as shown in Figure 2-4. You don't know the exact name of the company; all you know is that Barragan is part of the name.

6. Type ***Barragan*** and press Enter.

dBASE locates the record.

7. Press Tab to move the cursor to the address field.

8. Type **92 Espanola Way** and use Del to remove characters remaining from the old address.

Now you will change another record. At Tatlin Construction, the contact person Vlade has retired and has been replaced by Sarunas.

Figure 2-3

This is what you see when you first open the CUS-TOMRS data file using the CUSTFORM data entry form.

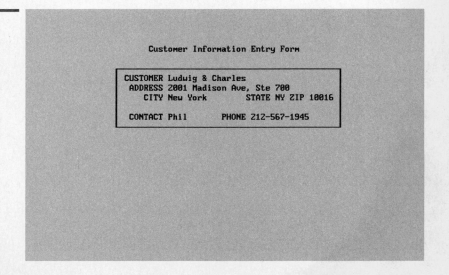

Customer Information Entry Form

CUSTOMER Ludwig & Charles
ADDRESS 2001 Madison Ave, Ste 700
    CITY New York   STATE NY ZIP 10016

CONTACT Phil   PHONE 212-567-1945

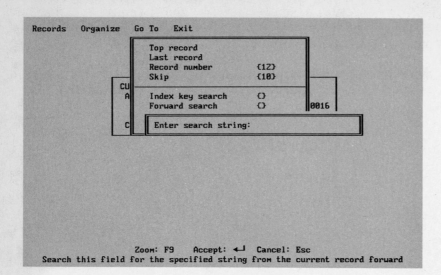

Figure 2-4

Enter a search string in the fill-in box to search for a record.

9. Press ↓ to move the cursor to the CONTACT field.

10. Press F10.

11. Choose Forward Search from the Go To menu.

    The fill-in box appears.

12. Type **Vlade** and press Enter.

    dBASE finds the record for Tatlin Construction.

13. Type **Sarunas**

    You are finished making changes.

14. Press F10.

15. Choose Exit from the Exit menu.

    You return to the Control Center. Now you will print a quick report so you can have a hard copy of the changes you made. Be sure the printer is turned on.

16. Press Shift-F9 (Quick Report).

17. Choose Begin Printing.

    The report prints.

Deleting Obsolete Records

If all the information in a record has to be changed, you may find it convenient to use the Blank Record command from the Records menu. This wipes out all the data in the current record and leaves it empty; however, the record is still there.

Sometimes, however, you may want to remove records altogether. Perhaps a client has gone out of business, or an employee is no longer with the company. If you wish to remove a record from the database, you must use a two-step operation. dBASE purposely

Figure 2-5

Use the Records menu to mark a record for deletion, or just place the cursor in the record and press ⌜Ctrl⌝-U.

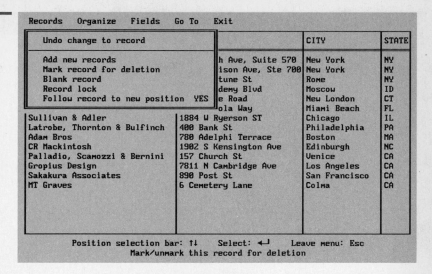

```
  Records   Organize   Fields   Go To   Exit
 ┌─────────────────────────────────────┐              ┌──────────┬──────┐
 │ Undo change to record               │              │CITY      │STATE │
 │                                     │              │          │      │
 │ Add new records                     │h Ave, Suite 570│New York│ NY   │
 │ Mark record for deletion            │ison Ave, Ste 700│New York│ NY   │
 │ Blank record                        │tune St       │Rome     │ NY   │
 │ Record lock                         │demy Blvd     │Moscow   │ ID   │
 │ Follow record to new position  YES  │e Road        │New London│ CT  │
 │                                     │ola Way       │Miami Beach│FL   │
 └─────────────────────────────────────┘
  Sullivan & Adler              1884 W Ryerson ST    Chicago       IL
  Latrobe, Thornton & Bulfinch  400 Bank St          Philadelphia  PA
  Adam Bros                     780 Adelphi Terrace  Boston        MA
  CR Mackintosh                 1902 S Kensington Ave Edinburgh    NC
  Palladio, Scamozzi & Bernini  157 Church St        Venice        CA
  Gropius Design                7811 N Cambridge Ave Los Angeles   CA
  Sakakura Associates           890 Post St          San Francisco CA
  MT Graves                     6 Cemetery Lane      Colma         CA

       Position selection bar: ↑↓   Select: ↵   Leave menu: Esc
                Mark/unmark this record for deletion
```

makes it a little harder to delete records, so that you will not do it by mistake. To delete a record, you must first mark it for deletion and then delete it with a pack command. To **pack** a database means to reduce it in size by deleting marked records.

To mark a record for deletion, go to the record and press ⌜Ctrl⌝-U. Alternatively, you can choose Mark Record for Deletion from the Records menu shown in Figure 2-5. If you have a number of records to delete, you can mark a series of records for deletion and then delete them all at once. You can even take your time to make sure that you want to delete them. After you mark a record for deletion, you can quit and restart dBASE and reopen the data file, and the record will still be marked. If you change your mind, you unmark a record by choosing Clear Delete Mark from the Records menu. Or, to unmark all marked records, choose Unmark All Records from the Organize menu shown in Figure 2-6.

Once records are marked, you pack the database by choosing Erase Marked Records from the Organize menu. Packing deletes marked records and renumbers the remaining ones.

Figure 2-6

Choose Unmark All Records from the Organize menu to unmark records slated for deletion before they are deleted.

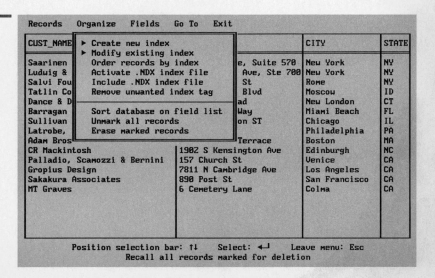

```
  Records   Organize   Fields   Go To   Exit
 ┌────────┬──────────────────────────────┐        ┌──────────┬──────┐
 │CUST_NAME│ ► Create new index          │        │CITY      │STATE │
 │         │ ► Modify existing index     │        │          │      │
 │Saarinen │   Order records by index    │e, Suite 570│New York│ NY │
 │Ludwig & │   Activate .NDX index file  │ Ave, Ste 700│New York│ NY│
 │Salvi Fou│   Include .NDX index file   │St        │Rome     │ NY  │
 │Tatlin Co│   Remove unwanted index tag │Blvd      │Moscow   │ ID  │
 │Dance & D│                             │ad        │New London│ CT │
 │Barragan │   Sort database on field list│Way      │Miami Beach│FL │
 │Sullivan │   Unmark all records        │on ST     │Chicago   │ IL │
 │Latrobe, │   Erase marked records      │          │Philadelphia│PA│
 │Adam Bros└──────────────────────────────┘Terrace  │Boston    │ MA │
 │CR Mackintosh                 1902 S Kensington Ave │Edinburgh │ NC │
 │Palladio, Scamozzi & Bernini  157 Church St        │Venice    │ CA │
 │Gropius Design                7811 N Cambridge Ave │Los Angeles│CA │
 │Sakakura Associates           890 Post St          │San Francisco│CA│
 │MT Graves                     6 Cemetery Lane      │Colma     │ CA │

       Position selection bar: ↑↓   Select: ↵   Leave menu: Esc
                Recall all records marked for deletion
```

Delete Records

Now you will use search commands to find records in the CUSTOMRS database, and then you will mark them for deletion and pack the database. Make sure you are working in drive A, your work disk is in drive A, and the cursor is at the Control Center.

1. Activate the CUSTFORM data entry form.

2. Press F2.

    The Edit screen appears. (If the Browse screen appears, press F2 again.)

The Graves company and the Dance company are going belly up, and you will mark their records for deletion from the file.

3. With the cursor in the customer field, press F10.

4. Choose Forward Search from the Go To menu.

5. Type ***Graves*** and press Enter.

    dBASE locates the record.

6. Press F10.

7. Choose Mark Record for Deletion from the Records menu.

As Figure 2-7 shows, the Del indicator appears to show that the record is marked for deletion.

8. Press F10.

9. Choose Forward Search from the Go To menu.

10. Type ***Dance*** and press Enter.

    dBASE finds the record for Dance & Dance, Architects.

11. Press Ctrl-U to mark the record for deletion.

12. Press Alt-E and choose Exit to return to the Control Center.

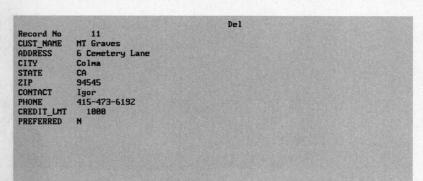

```
                                    Del
Record No       11
CUST_NAME    MT Graves
ADDRESS      6 Cemetery Lane
CITY         Colma
STATE        CA
ZIP          94545
CONTACT      Igor
PHONE        415-473-6192
CREDIT_LMT   1000
PREFERRED    N
```

Figure 2-7

The Del indicator shows that this record is marked for deletion; in the custom data entry screen the Del indicator appears at the bottom.

13. Press Alt-E to exit, and choose Quit to DOS.

You return to the DOS prompt.

The phone rings. It's Dance & Dance, saying they just got a contract to build a new base-ball stadium in San Francisco and are not going out of business after all.

14. Restart dBASE.

15. At the dot prompt, type **USE CUSTOMRS** and press Enter.

16. Type **SET FORM TO CUSTFORM** and press Enter.

17. Type **EDIT** and press Enter.

The Edit screen appears.

18. Repeat steps 8–10 to move the record pointer to the record for Dance & Dance, Architects.

dBASE finds the record. Note that it is still marked for deletion. Now you will unmark it.

19. Press F10.

20. Move the cursor to open the Records menu.

Note that the Mark Record for Deletion command now reads Clear Deletion Mark, as shown in Figure 2-8.

21. Highlight Clear Deletion Mark and press Enter to unmark the record. (You can also press Ctrl-U to unmark a marked record.)

Now you will pack the database to remove MT Graves, which is still marked for deletion.

22. Press F10.

23. Choose Erase Marked Records from the Organize menu.

dBASE asks if you are sure you want to erase all marked records.

24. Press Y to choose Yes.

Figure 2-8

When a record is already marked for deletion, the Mark Record for Deletion command changes to Clear Deletion Mark.

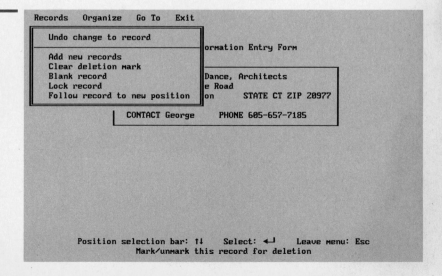

The database is packed.

25. Press F2.

The Browse screen, shown in Figure 2-9, shows the results: MT Graves is gone forever, and the remaining records are renumbered. Next, you will print a quick report.

26. Press Alt -E, E to return to the Control Center.

27. Press Shift - F9 (Quick Report).

28. Choose Begin Printing.

The report prints.

Sorting Records

Rearranging records in a database is one way of acquiring information from it. If you were to reorder a database alphabetically by city, for example, you could see at a glance all the customers from a given city. The natural order of the database would not show this. You could also reorder the records by the amount of money spent, to see who your best customers are, or by date, to see how business is going at different times of the year.

There are two ways to change the order of the records in a database: by indexing and by sorting. A **sort** physically reorders the records on the disk. You then copy them to another file and renumber them permanently. When you add records to a sorted file, they are added at the end. Whatever criterion you used to sort the file initially is no longer in force. dBASE performs a sort in **dictionary order**. This means that it follows the conventions of the English language: upper- and lowercase are considered the same. In dictionary order, de Falla comes before Dracula.

To sort a database, you use the Sort Database on Field List command under the Organize menu. A window appears, shown in Figure 2-10, in which you list the fields you want to sort on. The first field you list will be the primary sort. The ones below it are secondary. This means that dBASE sorts records on the primary field first. If there is more

CUST_NAME	ADDRESS	CITY	STATE
CR Mackintosh	1902 S Kensington Ave	Edinburgh	NC
Palladio, Scamozzi & Bernini	157 Church St	Venice	CA
Gropius Design	7811 N Cambridge Ave	Los Angeles	CA
Latrobe, Thornton & Bulfinch	400 Bank St	Philadelphia	PA
Tatlin Construction	1300 Academy Blvd	Moscow	ID
Saarinen & Son	611 Fifth Ave, Suite 570	New York	NY
Sullivan & Adler	1884 W Ryerson ST	Chicago	IL
Salvi Fountain Specialties	1732 Neptune St	Rome	NY
Barragan Associates	92 Espanola Way	Miami Beach	FL
Dance & Dance, Architects	1 Newgate Road	New London	CT
Ludwig & Charles	2001 Madison Ave, Ste 700	New York	NY
Sakakura Associates	890 Post St	San Francisco	CA
Adam Bros	780 Adelphi Terrace	Boston	MA

Figure 2-9

The database, minus one record, after the MT Graves record has been marked for deletion and the pack command has been issued.

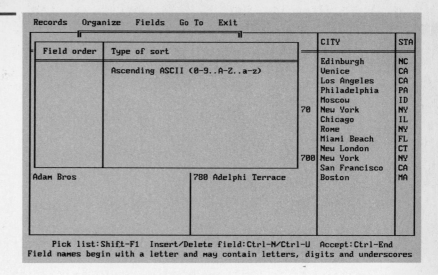

Figure 2-10

List the fields you want to sort on here; the first field listed will be the primary sort field.

than one record with identical data in that field, the records will be sorted by the next sort criterion.

For example, if you had a list of people and sorted on last name, what if there were ten people named Smith? You could have all the Smiths listed alphabetically by first name. Or if you sorted first by city, there might be hundreds of entries in the same city. You might want the secondary criterion to be zip code, or last name. In addition to specifying the field you want to sort on in the sort window, you also specify whether you want the sort to be in **ascending** (a–z, 0–9) or **descending** (z–a, 9–0) **order**. In case you forget what all the fields in the database are, press [Shift]-[F1], and dBASE presents you with a pick list of the fields, as shown in Figure 2-11.

Of course, always keep in mind that you can sort on first and last names only if you planned ahead and entered them in separate fields.

After you finish picking your sort criteria, press [Ctrl]-[End]. dBASE prompts you for the name of the file you want to save to. Type the name and press [Enter]. If you use a name that already exists, you will be asked if you want to **overwrite** the file. After the file is

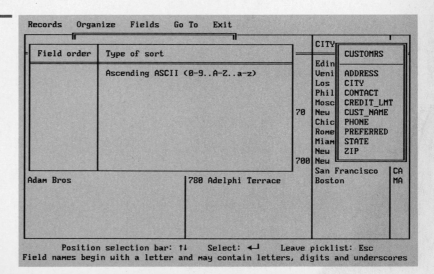

Figure 2-11

Press [Shift]-[F1] to see a pick list of fields available to sort on.

```
 Layout   Organize   Append   Go To   Exit              10:16:13 pm
                                           Bytes remaining:   3903
 ┌─────┬─────────────┬─────────────┬────────┬─────┬────────┐
 │ Num │ Field Name  │ Field Type  │ Width  │ Dec │ Index  │
 ├─────┼─────────────┼─────────────┼────────┼─────┼────────┤
 │  1  │ CUSTOMR     │ Character   │  30    │     │   Y    │
 │  2  │ ADDRESS     │ Character   │  25    │     │   N    │
 │  3  │ CITY        │ Character   │  15    │     │   Y    │
 │  4  │ STATE       │ Character   │   2    │     │   Y    │
 │  5  │ ZIP         │ Character   │   5    │     │   Y    │
 │  6  │ SALESPRSN   │ Character   │   3    │     │   N    │
 │  7  │ PART_NO     │ Character   │   5    │     │   Y    │
 │  8  │ QUANTITY    │ Numeric     │   4    │  0  │   N    │
 │  9  │ ORD_DATE    │ Date        │   8    │     │   N    │
 │     │             │             │        │     │        │
 └─────┴─────────────┴─────────────┴────────┴─────┴────────┘
 Database│A:\ORDRS            │Field 1/9     │          │
        Enter the field name.  Insert/Delete field:Ctrl-N/Ctrl-U
 Field names begin with a letter and may contain letters, digits and underscores
```

Figure 2-12

You can sort the ORDRS database from the design screen.

sorted into a new file, you will have two versions of the same database, with the records in different orders.

Sort Records

Now you will sort the records of the ORDRS database that you created in the application project at the end of Lesson 1. If you did not do this exercise, do it now. You will sort customer orders by date. Make sure you are working in drive A, your work disk is in drive A, and the cursor is at the Control Center.

1. Activate the ORDRS database.

2. Press [Shift]-[F2].

   The design screen appears, as in Figure 2-12.

3. Press [→] to open the Organize menu.

4. Choose Sort Database on Field List.

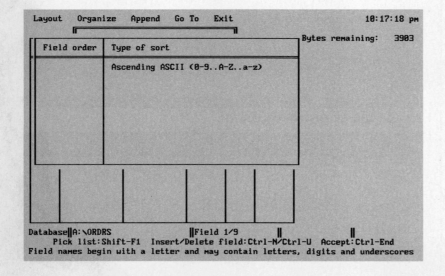

```
 Layout   Organize   Append   Go To   Exit              10:17:18 pm
      ┌────────────────────────────────┐  Bytes remaining:   3903
 ┌────┴───────────┬────────────────────┴────────────────────────┐
 │ Field order    │ Type of sort                                 │
 ├────────────────┼──────────────────────────────────────────────┤
 │                │ Ascending ASCII (0-9..A-Z..a-z)              │
 │                │                                              │
 │                │                                              │
 │                │                                              │
 │                │                                              │
 │                │                                              │
 └────────────────┴──────────────────────────────────────────────┘
 ┌────────┬────────┬────────┬────────┬────────┐
 │        │        │        │        │        │
 │        │        │        │        │        │
 │        │        │        │        │        │
 └────────┴────────┴────────┴────────┴────────┘
 Database│A:\ORDRS            │Field 1/9     │          │
     Pick list:Shift-F1   Insert/Delete field:Ctrl-N/Ctrl-U   Accept:Ctrl-End
 Field names begin with a letter and may contain letters, digits and underscores
```

Figure 2-13

List the fields you want to sort on in the sort window.

The sort window appears, as shown in Figure 2-13.

5. Press Shift-F1.

A pick list of fields appears.

6. Move the cursor to SALESPRSN and press Enter.

SALESPERSN appears in the sort window. The default is ascending order. Now you will define the secondary sort field.

7. Press ↓.

8. Press Shift-F1.

9. Move the cursor to ORD_DATE and press Enter.

ORD_DATE appears in the sort window. The default is ascending order.

10. Press Ctrl-End to accept the criteria.

dBASE asks for the name of the file you want to save to.

11. Type **a:custords** and press Enter.

dBASE sorts and renumbers the records to CUSTORDS, then prompts you for a description of the new file.

12. Type a description of your choice and press Enter.

13. Press Alt-E, Enter.

dBASE takes you to the Control Center. Figure 2-14 shows that CUSTORDS is now listed in the Data panel.

14. Move the cursor to CUSTORDS in the Data panel and press F2.

If the Edit screen appears, press F2 again to see the Browse screen. As Figure 2-15 shows, the customer order data file has been reordered by salesperson's initials and for each salesperson by date.

Figure 2-14

The Control Center, with CUSTORDS listed.

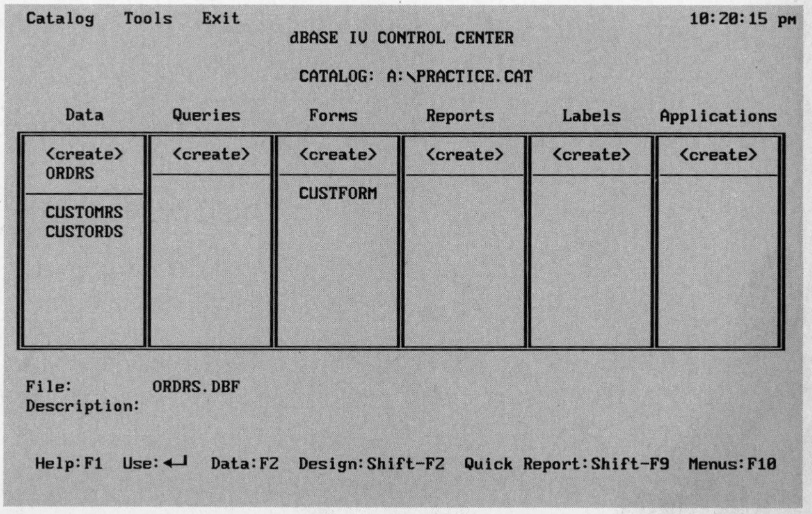

```
 Catalog   Tools   Exit                                      10:20:15 pm
                         dBASE IV CONTROL CENTER
                         CATALOG: A:\PRACTICE.CAT

     Data       Queries       Forms      Reports      Labels     Applications
  ┌──────────┬───────────┬───────────┬───────────┬───────────┬────────────┐
  │ <create> │ <create>  │ <create>  │ <create>  │ <create>  │ <create>   │
  │ ORDRS    │           │           │           │           │            │
  │          │           │ CUSTFORM  │           │           │            │
  │ CUSTOMRS │           │           │           │           │            │
  │ CUSTORDS │           │           │           │           │            │
  │          │           │           │           │           │            │
  │          │           │           │           │           │            │
  │          │           │           │           │           │            │
  │          │           │           │           │           │            │
  └──────────┴───────────┴───────────┴───────────┴───────────┴────────────┘

  File:        ORDRS.DBF
  Description:


   Help:F1  Use:↵  Data:F2  Design:Shift-F2  Quick Report:Shift-F9  Menus:F10
```

CITY	STATE	ZIP	SALESPRSN	PART_NO	QUANTITY	ORD_DATE
			HCD	10013	16	03/24/94
			HCD	10001	3	03/29/94
			JLH	10011	3	03/21/94
			JLH	10006	3	03/21/94
			JLH	10001	2	03/28/94
			JLH	10010	6	03/28/94
			LWB	10008	3	03/23/94
			LWB	10014	1	03/23/94
			LWB	10009	3	03/23/94
			NMC	10011	24	03/24/94
			NMC	10013	6	03/28/94
			NMC	10014	4	03/28/94
			NMC	10014	14	04/01/94
			PHC	10015	24	03/22/94
			PHC	10003	6	03/29/94
			PHC	10010	12	03/29/94
			TRL	10002	6	03/22/94
			TRL	10007	12	03/25/94

Figure 2-15

You sorted the customer orders file by salesperson's initials and saved the reordered file as CUSTORDS.DBF.

15. Press [Esc] to go back to the Control Center.
16. Press [Shift]-[F9] to print a quick report.
17. Choose Begin Printing.

    The report prints.

Creating Indexes

Indexes are more sophisticated and more powerful than sorting. An **index** is a file that dBASE uses to arrange records in a certain way that you define. With indexes, you can temporarily reorder records using several criteria, as with a sort. However, indexing does not actually change the natural order of the records in the database; it just gives you a look at them in a different order. Use a different index, and dBASE reorders the records again. Once you define an index, dBASE will save it so that you can use it over and over.

Unlike a sort, an index reorders all the records in a database, even if they were added after the index was created. Another way indexes are different from sorts is that they order records in **ASCII order** rather than dictionary order. ASCII order recognizes uppercase letters as coming before lowercase. In ASCII order, Dracula comes before de Falla.

There are two ways of creating indexes. The simplest way is one that you have already used. This consists of just placing a **Y** under Index when you are defining the fields of the database. When you do this, dBASE automatically creates a simple index in ascending ASCII order for that field and saves it.

You can, however, create much more sophisticated indexes by using the Organize menu on the database design screen, the Edit screen, or the Browse screen. Choose the Create New Index command, and a dialog box appears, as shown in Figure 2-16, asking you for a name for the index and a definition. To define the index, you must create an expression, known as a **key**, consisting of the names of the fields you want to index on. Once again, you can use [Shift]-[F1] to display the fields and choose the ones you want. You can

Figure 2-16

In this dialog box you define expressions to index the records of a data file.

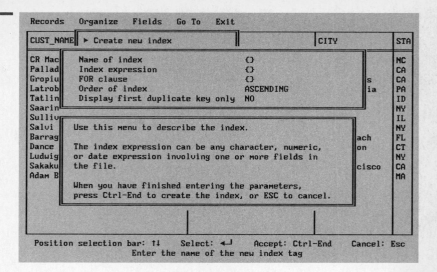

also type them in. The names are chained together, or concatenated, and joined by a plus sign. Figure 2-17 shows this box. You can only **concatenate** fields of the same type.

The index dialog box gives you more options for building an indexing expression. You can set the order of the index to acsending or descending, as with a sort.

The FOR clause is a powerful option that allows you to limit the index to certain records. You create an **expression** by using **restrictions**, **logical operators**, and **conditions** (the nouns and verbs of dBASE command language) much as you would at the dot prompt.

For example, if you wanted to see customers from California listed in alphabetical order, you would first index in ascending order on the CUST_NAME field. Then, in the FOR clause box, you would enter the expression **STATE = "CA"** where **STATE** is the restriction, = is the logical operator, and **"CA"** is the condition. dBASE would then display only those records in which the STATE field meets the condition CA. In a character field, you must surround the condition with quotation marks. Do not use quotes with a numerical field.

Figure 2.17

dBASE is set to index all records where "CA" appears in the STATE field, in ascending order according to the CUST_NAME field.

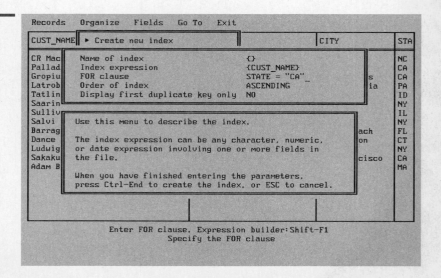

An additional option is Display First Duplicate Key Only. This command makes it possible to avoid the repetition of the data in a field. For example, if you index on the CITY field and dBASE groups all the records according to city, there may be 20 records with New York. If Display First Duplicate Key Only is on, only the first record will display the data New York. The subsequent records with New York in the CITY field will have that field blank. Eliminating this needless repetition makes for an easier-to-read display.

dBASE prompts you to name the index you created, and this name is called a **tag**. When you use the index, you choose the Order Records by Index command under the Organize menu and choose a tag name from the pick list that appears.

Create an Index

Now you will create an index to reorder the records of the HITTERS database, which you created in the application project at the end of Lesson 1. If you have not done this project, do it now. You will index ballplayers by league, team, and last name. In addition, you will restrict the display to show only hitters with over 300 at bats. Make sure you are working in drive A, your work disk is in drive A, and the cursor is at the Control Center.

1. Activate the HITTERS database.

2. Press [Shift]-[F2].

The design screen appears. (You can also do this exercise from the Edit or Browse screen.)

3. Press [Alt]-O to open the Organize menu (if it isn't already open).

4. With the highlight on Create New Index, press [Enter].

The index dialog box appears, as shown in Figure 2-18. First, you will give the index a tag.

5. With the highlight on Name of Index, press [Enter] to activate the fill-in box.

6. Type **bigbats** and press [Enter] again.

Next, you will choose the fields to index on. The cursor should be on Index Expression.

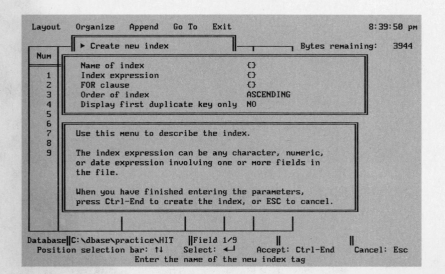

Figure 2-18

You can also open the index dialog box from the data design screen.

Figure 2-19

Press [Shift]-[F1] to see a pick list of all fields, as well as a list of operators and functions.

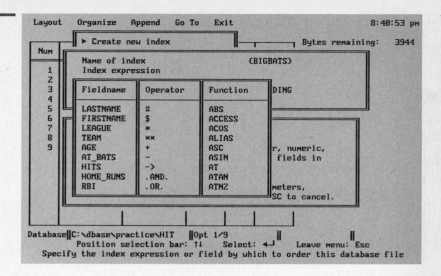

---

7. Press [Enter] to activate the fill-in box.

8. Press [Shift]-[F1] to see a pick list of fields.

The pick list appears, as shown in Figure 2-19.

9. Move the cursor to LEAGUE and press [Enter].

*The word **league** appears in the index expression. Now you will choose a secondary field to sort on, but first you must add a plus (+) sign.*

10. Type +

11. Press [Shift]-[F1] to pick another field.

12. Choose TEAM.

*The word **team** now appears after **league**, joined by a plus (+) sign. Now you will add another secondary field.*

13. Type +

Figure 2-20

The expression on the right will index records in ascending order by league, team, and last name.

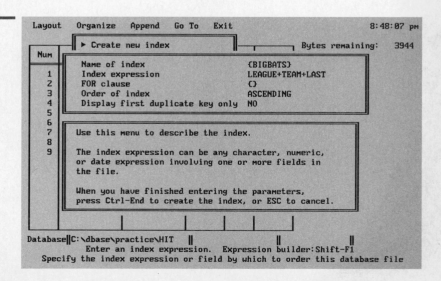

Figure 2-31

This is how the report looks after adding the footer.

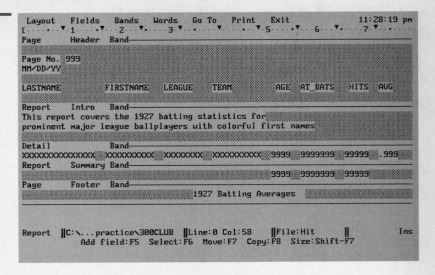

The finished report should look like Figure 2-32. Make any necessary adjustments now. After making changes, you will print the report.

27. Press [Alt]-P and choose Begin Printing.

The report prints.

28. Press [Alt]-E and then press [Enter] to save your work and return to the Control Center.

Queries

As unglamorous as database work may seem, Hollywood has managed to present it with flair and drama. Movie viewers will no doubt remember that typically electrifying moment in their favorite techno-thriller when a computer solves in seconds an enigma that has baffled everyone throughout the film. The protagonist says something like "Let's see how many were born before 1964, in any state north of the 42nd parallel, and have a scar on the left cheek." The computer whirs, buzzes, and displays a flurry of data. "Alright, now let's see which ones tested positive for factor X." At the keyboard, the

Figure 2-32

The completed batting averages report should look like this.

```
Page No.    1
08/16/93

LASTNAME        FIRSTNAME   LEAGUE    TEAM         AGE   AT_BATS   HITS   AVG

This report covers the 1927 batting statistics for
prominent major league ballplayers with colorful first names

Ruth            Babe        American  Yankees      32     540      192   .356
Cobb            Ty          American  Athletics    40     490      175   .357
Branom          Dud         American  Athletics    29      94       22   .234
Jacobson        Baby Doll   American  Athletics    36      35        8   .229
Goslin          Goose       American  Senators     26     581      194   .334
Ruel            Muddy       American  Senators     31     428      132   .308
Stewart         Stuffy      American  Senators     33     129       31   .240
Rigney          Topper      American  Senators     30     132       36   .273
Thurston        Sloppy      American  Senators     28      92       29   .315
Manush          Heinie      American  Tigers       25     593      177   .298
Ussat           Dutch       American  Indians      23      16        3   .188
Wanninger       Pee Wee     American  Red Sox      24      60       12   .200
Traynor         Pie         National  Pirates      27     573      196   .342
Toporcer        Specs       National  Cardinals    28     290       72   .248
Maranville      Rabbit      National  Cardinals    35      29        7   .241
                Cancel viewing: ESC,  Continue viewing: SPACEBAR
```

computer operator pushes his glasses back on his nose and taps a few more keys. Everyone waits a few suspense-filled seconds, and magically, from billions of pieces of information, the answer emerges. The reason it takes an hour and a half of screen time to get the answer is that that is how long it takes the humans to figure out the question. The rest is easy.

The interaction we just described taking place between humans and computers is known as a query. A **query** is like a question, or series of questions, you ask dBASE in order to search a database and see only those records that meet your criteria.

You want to know who your best customer is in terms of total sales for the past five years? Create a query. You want to know which state most of your customers are located in? How many spend over $50,000 with you? You find the answers to these questions with queries, provided of course that the information necessary to answer the questions is in the database.

To answer these types of questions, you are going to use a method known as **query by example (QBE)**. You can perform a query by example from the Control Center. First, activate the database you want to query. Then choose <create> in the Queries panel. The query design screen, shown in Figure 2-33, appears. Like other design screens, the query screen has a menu bar at the top with some of the usual **pull-down menus**. At the bottom of the screen are the status bar, navigation line, and message line.

The work surface is a bit different. Below the menu bar is the **file skeleton**. The file skeleton lists, from left to right, the name of the current database and then names for each field of the database. It is, in essence, a list from which you choose. Near the bottom of the screen, just above the status bar, is the **view skeleton**. This lists the fields you are going to see. At first, all the fields are listed. To restrict the view, you delete fields from the view skeleton. You can also move fields around for a better display. You move the cursor to the right across the skeletons by pressing (Tab) and to the left by pressing (Shift)-(Tab). To move between skeletons, press (F3) (Previous) and (F4) (Next). The work surface between the file and view skeletons is where you see the data displayed.

Let's take a simple example, the CUSTOMRS database. If you want to see only the customers in California, you type **"CA"** in the STATE field of the file skeleton. Character

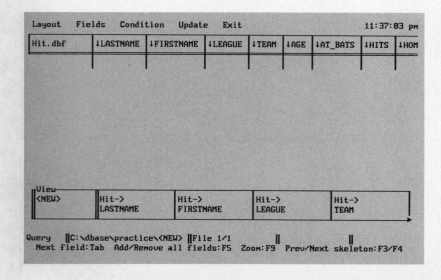

Figure 2-33

The query design screen shows the file skeleton (top) and the view skeleton (bottom).

values must be enclosed in double quotation marks. Then press [F2] (Data). dBASE searches the database and displays the Browse screen with only those records that meet the condition you specified. To return to the query design screen, press [Shift]-[F2]. You can continue to write conditions into the fields of the view skeleton to narrow the display.

Those fields of the file skeleton that are displayed in the view skeleton have a downward-pointing arrow. This is to remind you of what is being displayed. It is not necessary, however, for a field in which you are typing a condition to be displayed in the view skeleton. For ease of reading, you may decide to eliminate all fields in the view skeleton except CUST_NAME. You can still go to the file skeleton and enter conditions into any field, whether they are displayed or not.

To delete a field from the view skeleton, move the cursor to the view skeleton by pressing [F4] (Next). Then, move the cursor to the field you want to remove and press [F5], or choose Remove Field from View from the Fields menu. To move a field in the view skeleton, highlight it, press [F6] (Extend Select), press [F7] (Move), and then use [Tab] and [Shift]-[Tab] to move to the right or left. To add a deleted field back to the view skeleton, press [F4] (Next) to move the cursor back to the file skeleton. Highlight the field you want to add and press [F5], or choose Add Field to View from the Fields menu.

To specify a condition in a character field, move the cursor to the field you want in the file skeleton. Type the value you are looking for, such as **"Miami"** in the CITY field or **"CA"** in the STATE field, and press [F2]. You can use wild-card characters such as the asterisk (*), as you did in creating indexes. You can also search numeric, logic, and date fields. The values in a date field must be enclosed in curly brackets {}. In a logic field, it's **.T.** for true, or **.F.** for false. To remove a value, press [Ctrl]-Y.

If you are searching for a specific value, queries are easy enough: just type the value in the field of the file skeleton. But what if you want to know more? You may want to ask questions that involve several questions at once, such as: which customers from New York and California spent over $10,000 last year? dBASE has a battery of tools you can use to put together more complex queries.

Relational operators are one such tool. The table below of relational operators shows what they mean in a conditional expression.

=	equal to
>	greater than
<	less than
=>	equal to or greater than
=<	equal to or less than
<> or #	not equal to
$	includes

The operator **$** helps you find a value embedded within text or numbers, without having to specify the place as you do with wild cards. For example, to find all customers with the letters **Ltd** in the name, type **$ "Ltd"** in the CUST_NAME field of the file skeleton.

Keep in mind that dBASE differentiates upper and lower case; with the above criteria, it will not find the letters **ltd**.

Specify a Range

To specify a range of values for dBASE to search within, enter the lower and upper values in the range. For example, to find customers with credit limits between $3,000 and $5,000, type **>3000, <5000** in the CREDIT_LMT field of the file skeleton, as shown in Figure 2-34.

AND/OR Conditions

Sometimes you are searching for more than one value. There are several possibilities. If you want to find all customers in California with a credit limit over $5,000, you should know by now how to do that. Specify **"CA"** in the STATE field, and **5000** in the CREDIT_LMT field. This combining of values in two different fields is treated as an AND search. That is, the records must meet both the first criterion *and* the second criterion. You can specify values like this in every field; dBASE treats them as an AND search.

Sometimes, however, you may want to find records that meet either one criterion *or* another, in the same field or in separate fields. For example, you may want to locate a customer whose name you can't remember but who you know is located in either North Carolina or Virginia. To search for either one value or another, place one value in the appropriate field in the file skeleton. Then, press ↓ to add a line to the file skeleton and enter the second condition in the second line, as shown in Figure 2-35. You can combine AND and OR queries in the same field or in separate fields.

You can also add **summary operators** as a condition or part of a condition. The table below shows what the summary operators are and what result they give:

SUM   The total of all the values in the field

AVG or AVERAGE   The total of all the values in the field divided by the number of records

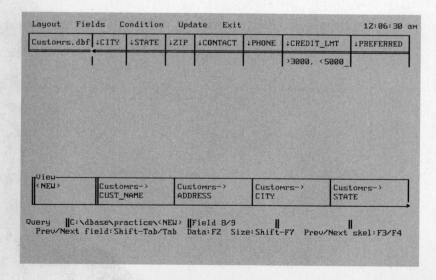

Figure 2-34

The expression on the left means "Find all records with a credit limit between three and five thousand dollars."

Figure 2-35

Setting up a search for one value OR another

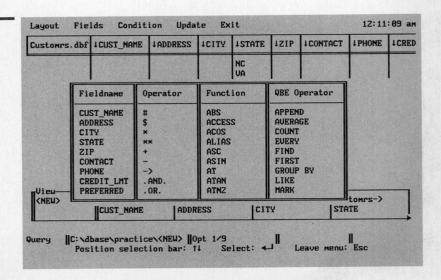

```
 Layout  Fields  Condition  Update  Exit                    12:08:58 am
┌─────────────────────────────────────────────────────────────────────┐
│Customrs.dbf ↓CUST_NAME │↓ADDRESS │↓CITY │↓STATE │↓ZIP │↓CONTACT │↓PHONE │↓CRED│
│                                          NC                           │
│                                          VA                           │
│                                                                       │
│ View                                                                  │
│ <NEW>       Customrs->   Customrs->   Customrs->   Customrs->         │
│             CUST_NAME    ADDRESS      CITY         STATE              │
│                                                                       │
 Query   ║C:\dbase\practice\<NEW> ║Field 4/9        ║           ║
         Prev/Next field:Shift-Tab/Tab  Data:F2  Size:Shift-F7  Prev/Next skel:F3/F4
```

MIN	The smallest value in the field
MAX	The largest value in the field
CNT or COUNT	A count of the records

You can combine summary operators with AND conditions. To find the average credit limit of all customers in California, for example, you would type **AVG** in the CREDIT_LMT field and **"CA"** in the STATE field.

The Group By command allows you to group records by a condition. For example, if you type **AVG** in the CREDIT_LMT field and **GROUP BY** in the STATE field, dBASE gives you the average credit for every state.

If you forget what all the expressions are or what the exact spelling of an expression is, you can press Shift-F1 to open the Expression Builder menu, shown in Figure 2-36. Highlight the expression with the cursor and press Enter.

Figure 2-36

Press Shift-F1 to see the Expression Builder menu, in case you forget the exact spelling of an expression.

```
 Layout  Fields  Condition  Update  Exit                    12:11:09 am
┌─────────────────────────────────────────────────────────────────────┐
│Customrs.dbf ↓CUST_NAME │↓ADDRESS │↓CITY │↓STATE │↓ZIP │↓CONTACT │↓PHONE │↓CRED│
│                                          NC                           │
│                                          VA                           │
│    ┌──────────┬──────────┬──────────┬──────────┐                     │
│    │ Fieldname│ Operator │ Function │ QBE Operator│                   │
│    │ CUST_NAME│  #       │ ABS      │ APPEND     │                    │
│    │ ADDRESS  │  $       │ ACCESS   │ AVERAGE    │                    │
│    │ CITY     │  *       │ ACOS     │ COUNT      │                    │
│    │ STATE    │  **      │ ALIAS    │ EVERY      │                    │
│    │ ZIP      │  +       │ ASC      │ FIND       │                    │
│    │ CONTACT  │  -       │ ASIN     │ FIRST      │                    │
│    │ PHONE    │  ->      │ AT       │ GROUP BY   │                    │
│    │ CREDIT_LMT│ .AND.   │ ATAN     │ LIKE       │                    │
│View│ PREFERRED│ .OR.     │ ATN2     │ MARK       │ tomrs->            │
│<NEW>└──────────┴──────────┴──────────┴──────────┘                     │
│          CUST_NAME    ADDRESS      CITY         STATE                 │
 Query   ║C:\dbase\practice\<NEW> ║Opt 1/9          ║           ║
         Position selection bar: ↑↓   Select: ↵   Leave menu: Esc
```

price for each is, how many are in stock, when to reorder, from whom, and for how much. Again, there is one record for each item. Finally, in the orders database, the company logs each order that comes in, who made the order and where the goods are to be sent, the price, who made the sale, and the quantity. In this database, there is one record per part number per customer. There is no way that all this information could be put into one database.

This all seems fairly logical. When you think about exactly what happens when an order comes in, however, this arrangement leaves a few gaps. First, an order requires that some information be entered into the order database; some, into the customer database; and some, into the inventory database.

If you want to create a sales report at the end of the month, you will actually have to create three reports. Think of the needless duplication involved in such an effort, to say nothing of the potential for errors when, for example, a customer's name has to be entered so many times.

The ideal situation would be for the three data files to be related somehow so that dBASE could use them all at once. This is what **relational databases** are all about. A relational database relates two or more data files so that you can use data on the basis of the relationship. Each database in a relational database system is sometimes called an **entity**. With a program like dBASE IV, you can create a lean, powerful relational database system, eliminating duplication in data entry and saving disk space. You can even change the relation between the entities easily as your needs change.

Building a relational database requires a bit more planning than creating just one data file. Before you begin, you must think of the end: what you need to get out of it. There are two main principles to keep in mind. First, the relationship between two databases must be based on a **common field**. For example, if you could relate the ORDRS database and the CUSTOMRS database, you wouldn't need to include the address, city, state, zip, and phone fields in the order database, because they are already in the customer database. All you need is one field in the order database to tell dBASE which customer, and the program will go find the rest. The customer name field could accomplish this. The drawback here, however, is that if each time an order is entered the customer name is not spelled precisely the same way, dBASE will not be able to match it to the record with the customer information in CUSTOMRS. It makes much more sense to assign a number to each customer, just as each part has a number in the STOCK database. It's much easier to get a five-digit number right than a long, complicated name.

The second principle in building a relational database is that there must be one **primary** or **controlling database** and that the others will be the controlled databases. In our scenario of separate data files for customers, inventory, and orders, which one should control, and which should be controlled? Since the entire process is set off each time an order is placed, common sense dictates that the ORDRS database be the controlling database. Each order must relate to CUSTOMRS to get customer information, and it must relate to STOCK to get part information. ORDRS and STOCK already have a field in common: the part number.

In the next section, you will actually link the three databases you have created, but first they must each be changed in order to be properly organized as part of a relational database.

Prepare a Relational Database

Now you will make changes in the CUSTOMRS, ORDRS, and STOCK databases and save them under new names. You will add a field for the customer number in both the customer and order data files. You will eliminate duplicate fields in the ORDRS database: CUST_NAME, ADDRESS, CITY, ZIP, PHONE, and PRICE. The STOCK database is OK the way it is. You will also create a new catalog, CUSTREQ, to keep the revamped data files.

Make sure you are working in drive A, your work disk is in drive A, and the cursor is at the Control Center.

1. Highlight CUSTOMRS in the Data panel and press [Enter].

2. Highlight Modify Structure and press [Enter].

The database design screen appears. First, you will save the database under a new name.

3. Press [Alt]-L and choose Save This Database Structure.

You are prompted for the name of the data file.

4. Type **a:clients** and press [Enter].

dBASE saves a copy of the file under the new name. The original CUSTOMRS data file is still intact. Next, you will add the customer number field.

5. With the cursor on the first line, press [Ctrl]-N to insert a field.

A blank field is added as the first field.

6. Under Field Name, type **CUST_NO** and press [Tab].

7. Make it a character field, five characters wide, and type **Y** to index.

Your screen should look like Figure 3-1. Next, you will assign each customer a number.

8. Press [Alt]-E, highlight Save Changes and Exit, and press [Enter] twice.

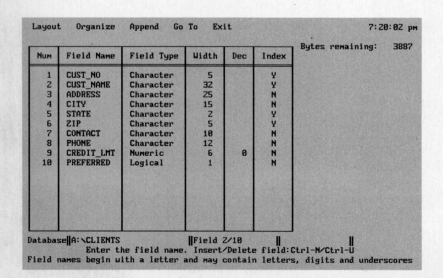

Figure 3-1

You will save the customer database under a new name and add a field for the customer number.

9. Press F2 to go to the Browse screen.

10. Enter a number for each customer as shown in the table below.

Number	Customer
10001	CR Mackintosh
10002	Palladio, Scamozzi & Bernini
10003	Gropius Design
10004	Latrobe, Thornton & Bulfinch
10005	Tatlin Construction
10006	Saarinen & Son
10007	Sullivan & Adler
10008	Salvi Fountain Specialties
10009	Barragan Associates
10010	Dance & Dance, Architects
10011	Ludwig & Charles
10012	Sakakura Associates
10013	Adam Bros

11. Press Alt-E, E to return to the Control Center.

Now you will print a quick report of CLIENTS.

12. Press Shift-F9 and choose Begin Printing.

The report prints. Save the printout as a reference. Next, you will make changes in the ORDRS data file.

13. Highlight ORDRS in the Data panel and press Enter.

14. Highlight Modify Structure and press Enter.

The structure of ORDRS appears on the database design screen. First, save a copy of the file under a new name.

15. Press Alt-L and choose Save This Database File Structure.

16. Type **a:requests**

dBASE saves the file as REQUESTS.DBF on your work disk. The original file, ORDRS, is still intact. Next, you will add the customer number field.

17. Repeat steps 5–8 to add the same customer number field, CUST_NO, to REQUESTS that you added to CLIENTS, and save the new structure.

18. Press F2 (Data) to see the Browse screen.

19. Using the printout of CLIENTS as a guide, fill in the appropriate number for each customer in each record.

20. Press Alt -E, Enter, Shift - F2.

You return to the design screen. Now you will eliminate the unnecessary fields from RE-QUESTS. It doesn't matter that the data in them will be wiped out, because the customer number and the part number are all you need.

21. With the cursor in the CUSTOMR field, press Ctrl -U to delete the field.

The field disappears; the remaining fields close up and are renumbered.

22. Repeat step 21 for the fields ADDRESS, CITY, STATE, ZIP, PHONE, and PRICE.

When you are through, your screen should look like Figure 3-2.

23. Press Alt -E and choose Save Changes and Exit.

24. Press Enter to return to the Control Center.

The STOCK data file is OK as is; you don't need to change anything. The only thing left to do is to create a new catalog for your relational database and assign the files to it.

25. Press Alt -C to open the Catalog menu.

26. Choose Use a Different Catalog and press Enter.

A pick list appears.

27. Choose <create>.

A fill-in box prompts you to name the new catalog.

28. Type **CUSTREQ** and press Enter.

The new catalog is created. Now you will assign the files for the relational database to it.

29. Press Alt -C and choose Add File to Catalog.

A pick list appears, showing the names of files you can add to the catalog.

30. Highlight CLIENTS and press Enter.

```
Layout   Organize   Append   Go To   Exit              7:56:29 pm
                                         Bytes remaining:   3975
 Num | Field Name | Field Type | Width | Dec | Index
  1    CUST_NO      Character      5            Y
  2    SALESPRSN    Character      3            N
  3    PART_NO      Character      5            Y
  4    QUANTITY     Numeric        4      0     N
  5    ORD_DATE     Date           8            N

Database||A:\REQUESTS          ||Field 2/5    ||          ||
          Enter the field name. Insert/Delete field:Ctrl-N/Ctrl-U
Field names begin with a letter and may contain letters, digits and underscores
```

Figure 3-2

You will save the order database under a new name and add fields for customer number and part number.

You are prompted for a description of the file.

31. Type **Customer List of Modern Architectural Supply** and press Enter.

32. Repeat steps 29–30 for REQUESTS and STOCK and write a description of your own choosing.

CLIENTS, REQUESTS, and STOCK are listed in the Data panel.

Using a Query to Create a Relational Database

In the previous exercise, you planned and designed your relational database. You laid the groundwork by conceiving REQUESTS as the controlling file, with CLIENTS and STOCK as the controlled files. You also made sure that REQUESTS had a common field with CLIENTS (the customer number field), as well as one with STOCK (the part number field). It helps to write down an outline of your relational database, so you can remember which fields in which files you want to link and how the files are related.

The only step remaining to bring the relational database into being is to link the files. That ever-handy dBASE feature, the query, is ready to assist you, for it is with queries that you link files into a relational database. Another aspect of queries, in addition to what you've already learned, is that a query can involve more than one file.

To link files, you begin by activating the controlling database: in our case, REQUESTS. Then you create a new query for it. At the query design screen, you choose Add File to Query from the Layout menu. A list box appears, as shown in Figure 3-3, asking which file you want to add. Choose the file you want to relate and press Enter. dBASE adds another file skeleton to the query screen, just below the main one, as shown in Figure 3-4. Continue to add the files you need.

When you have added all the files you want to relate (in our example, CLIENTS and STOCK), the next step is to actually establish the link. This is a simple matter of typing a phrase into each field the databases have in common. REQUESTS is related to CLIENTS through the customer number field. Therefore, to link them, type LINK1 in the

Figure 3-3

You create a query to link files into a relational database.

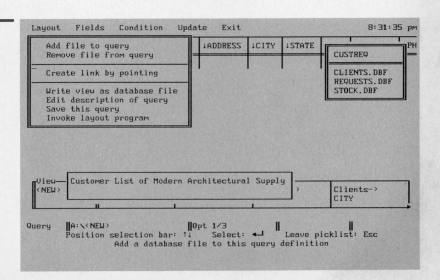

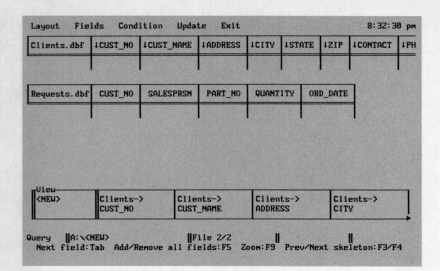

Figure 3-4

A query can use fields from more than one database.

CUST_NO field of REQUESTS and type LINK1 in the CUST_NO field of CLIENTS, as shown in Figure 3-5. Do the same thing to create another link between REQUESTS and STOCK. Type LINK2 in the PART_NO field of REQUESTS and type LINK2 in the PART_NO field of STOCK.

Another way to create a link is to choose the Create Link by Pointing command in the Layout menu, shown in Figure 3-6. You then move the cursor to the field you want in the first file and press (Enter). The phrase LINK1 appears. Then move the cursor to the field you want in the second file and press (Enter). The phrase appears again.

You don't have to type LINK1; you can use any word you want, as long as it is exactly the same in the two files you want to link. To finish out the query, you will probably want to adjust the number of fields in the view skeleton to display the information you want. This will make it easier to create a report based on this query later.

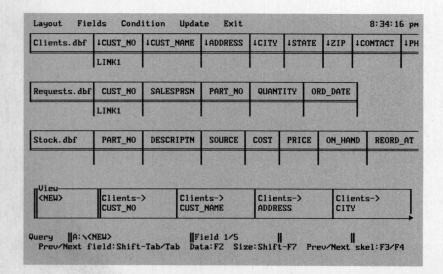

Figure 3-5

To link two data files, you must type a common word into a common field in a query.

Figure 3-6

You can also use the Create a Link by Pointing command to supply the common word to link two files.

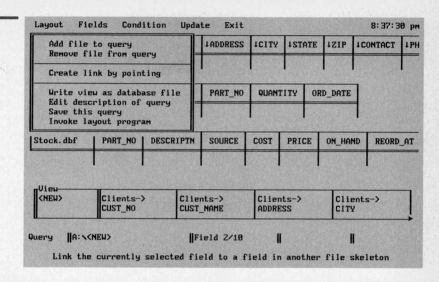

Use a Query to Link a Relational Database

Now you will create a query for the controlling file, REQUESTS, add the CLIENTS and STOCK files to the query, and link the related files with the Create Link by Pointing command.

You should be working in drive A, with your work disk in drive A, and the cursor at the Control Center. Make sure the current catalog is CUSTREQ.

1. Activate the REQUESTS data file.

2. Move the cursor to the <create> button in the Queries panel and press [Enter].

   The query design screen appears.

3. Press [Alt]-L to open the Layout menu (if it isn't already open).

4. Highlight Add File to Query and press [Enter].

   The pick list shown in Figure 3-7 opens, asking you to choose which file to add.

Figure 3-7

From the controlling data file, REQUESTS, you will add CLIENTS and STOCK to the query.

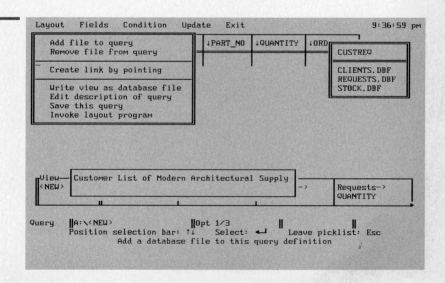

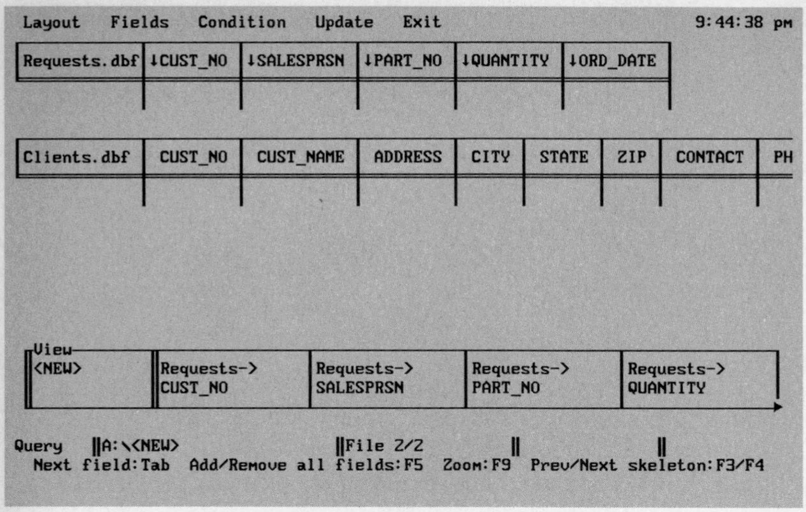

```
 Layout   Fields   Condition   Update   Exit                    9:44:38 pm
┌──────────┬────────┬──────────┬────────┬──────────┬─────────┐
│Requests.dbf│↓CUST_NO│↓SALESPRSN│↓PART_NO│↓QUANTITY│↓ORD_DATE│
├──────────┼────────┼──────────┼────────┼──────────┼─────────┤
│          │        │          │        │          │         │
└──────────┴────────┴──────────┴────────┴──────────┴─────────┘

┌──────────┬────────┬──────────┬────────┬──────┬──────┬─────┬─────────┬───┐
│Clients.dbf│CUST_NO│CUST_NAME│ADDRESS │CITY  │STATE │ZIP  │CONTACT  │PH │
├──────────┼────────┼──────────┼────────┼──────┼──────┼─────┼─────────┼───┤
│          │        │          │        │      │      │     │         │   │
└──────────┴────────┴──────────┴────────┴──────┴──────┴─────┴─────────┴───┘

┌View────────────────────────────────────────────────────────────┐
│<NEW>   ║Requests->  ║Requests->  ║Requests->  ║Requests->       │
│        ║CUST_NO     ║SALESPRSN   ║PART_NO     ║QUANTITY          │
└─────────────────────────────────────────────────────────────────>
 Query   ║A:\<NEW>         ║File 2/2   ║        ║
  Next field:Tab  Add/Remove all fields:F5  Zoom:F9  Prev/Next skeleton:F3/F4
```

Figure 3-8

The file skeleton from CLIENTS.DBF is added to the query.

5. Highlight CLIENTS.DBF and press (Enter).

The file skeleton for CLIENTS appears below the file skeleton for REQUESTS, as shown in Figure 3-8. Now you will link the two files.

6. Press (F3) (Previous) and (Tab) to move the cursor to the CUST_NO field of the REQUESTS file skeleton.

7. Press (Alt)-L to open the Layout menu.

8. Highlight Create Link by Pointing and press (Enter).

The word LINK1 appears in the CUST_NO field of REQUESTS, as shown in Figure 3-9. (Note that the message bar tells you to press (Enter) to finish the link.)

9. Press (F4) (Next) to move the cursor to the CLIENTS file skeleton.

10. With the cursor in the CUST_NO field, press (Enter).

LINK1 appears. The first link is complete. This is a good time to save your work.

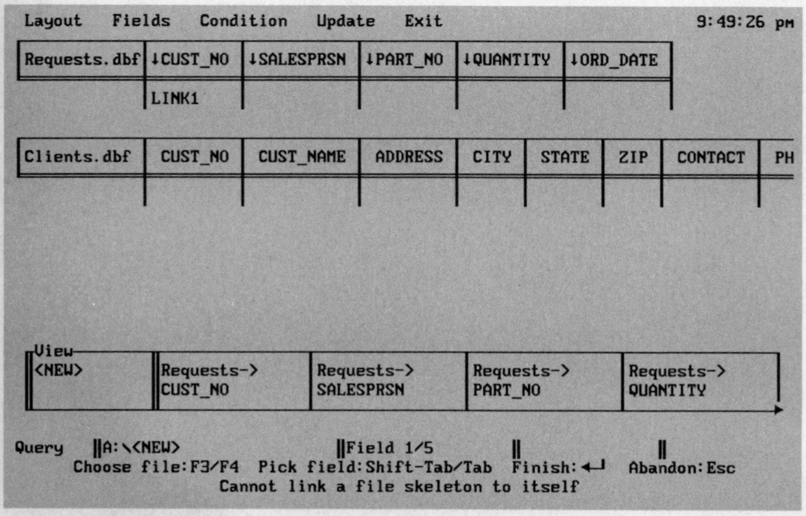

```
 Layout   Fields   Condition   Update   Exit                    9:49:26 pm
┌──────────┬────────┬──────────┬────────┬──────────┬─────────┐
│Requests.dbf│↓CUST_NO│↓SALESPRSN│↓PART_NO│↓QUANTITY│↓ORD_DATE│
├──────────┼────────┼──────────┼────────┼──────────┼─────────┤
│          │LINK1   │          │        │          │         │
└──────────┴────────┴──────────┴────────┴──────────┴─────────┘

┌──────────┬────────┬──────────┬────────┬──────┬──────┬─────┬─────────┬───┐
│Clients.dbf│CUST_NO│CUST_NAME│ADDRESS │CITY  │STATE │ZIP  │CONTACT  │PH │
├──────────┼────────┼──────────┼────────┼──────┼──────┼─────┼─────────┼───┤
│          │        │          │        │      │      │     │         │   │
└──────────┴────────┴──────────┴────────┴──────┴──────┴─────┴─────────┴───┘

┌View────────────────────────────────────────────────────────────┐
│<NEW>   ║Requests->  ║Requests->  ║Requests->  ║Requests->       │
│        ║CUST_NO     ║SALESPRSN   ║PART_NO     ║QUANTITY          │
└─────────────────────────────────────────────────────────────────>
 Query   ║A:\<NEW>         ║Field 1/5   ║        ║
  Choose file:F3/F4  Pick field:Shift-Tab/Tab  Finish:↵  Abandon:Esc
                    Cannot link a file skeleton to itself
```

Figure 3-9

When you issue the Create Link by Pointing command, the word LINK1 appears where you placed the cursor.

Figure 3-25

An empty pop-up menu waits for you to fill in the commands you want it to list.

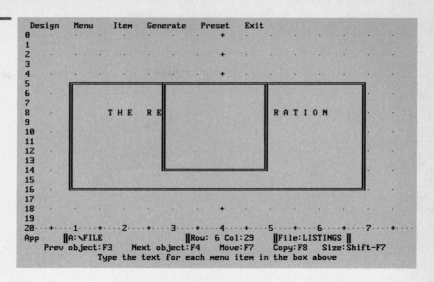

size of the menu box, if necessary. Then save the menu and choose Put Away Current Menu from the Menu menu.

To reopen the application definition screen from the dot prompt, the command is MODIFY APPLICATION <filename>. The command to run the application is DO <filename>.

Design Menus

Now you will use the dBASE IV Application Generator to design the menus for your application. You will create a main menu and three pop-up menus.

You should be working in drive A, with your work disk in drive A and the cursor at the dot prompt.

1. Type **modify application domail** and press Enter.

   The application definition screen appears.

2. Press Alt-D to open the Design menu.

3. Highlight Horizontal Bar Menu and press Enter.

   An empty list box appears.

4. Highlight <create> and press Enter.

   The menu dialog box appears.

5. In the Name box, type **mainmenu**

6. Press ↓ to move to the next line.

7. In the Description line, type **Choose File commands, Print commands,** or **Exit**

8. In the Message Line Prompt line, type **Use the arrow keys to select one of the menu options**

   Your dialog box should look like Figure 3-26.

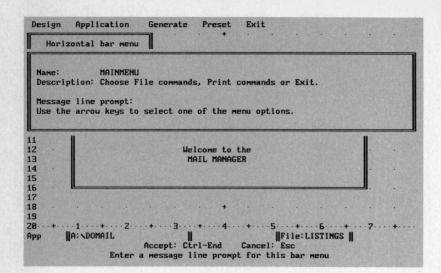

Figure 3-26

When you create your own menus, you can create any message prompt that you want.

9. Press Ctrl-End to save.

   The menu bar appears, ready for you to type in the name of each pop-up. The cursor should be at the first position of the bar.

10. Press F5, type **Files**, and press F5 again.

11. Move the cursor to column 28, press F5, type **Reports**, and press F5 again.

12. Press → to move the cursor to column 58.

13. Press F5, type **Exit**, and press F5 again.

    Your screen should look like Figure 3-27.

14. Save your work thus far by choosing Save Current Menu from the Menu menu.

    You have created the main menu bar for the DOMAIL application. Next, you will create the pop-up menus FILES and REPORTS.

15. Press F10 and choose Pop-up Menu from the Design menu.

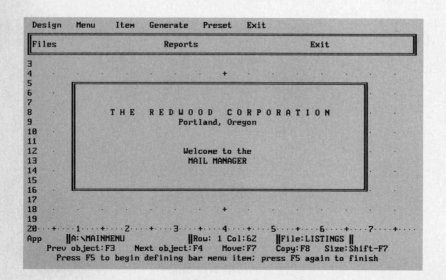

Figure 3-27

This is how your screen looks after you type the names of the three menus in the menu bar.

16. Choose <create>.

    The dialog box to define the pop-up menus appears.

17. Fill in the following information:

    Name: **FILES**

    Description: **This menu lets you view, add, edit, or delete records.**

    Message line prompt: **Use the arrow keys to select one of the menu options.**

18. Press [Ctrl]-[End].

    An empty pop-up menu appears, with the cursor in the upper left. Now you will enter the menu choices.

19. Type **Add a Record** and press [Enter].

20. Type the next three lines, pressing [Enter] after each one:

    Delete a Record

    Edit a Record

    Browse Records

    Your screen should look like Figure 3-28. Next you will size the menu box.

21. Press [Shift]-[F7].

    The menu box flashes on and off, indicating it is ready to be sized.

22. Press [↑] four times and press [Enter].

    The menu box is now the right size. Now you must place it.

23. Press [F7] (Move).

    A dialog box appears, asking if you want to move the entire frame or only an item.

24. Choose Entire Frame.

Figure 3-28

These are the four commands for the File menu you are creating.

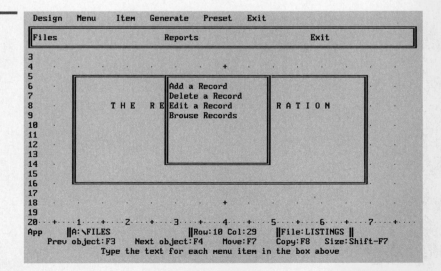

It flashes again.

25. Use the arrow keys to move the cursor to row 2, column 1 and press Enter.

The menu moves.

26. Choose Save Current Menu from the Menu menu.

27. Choose Put Away Current Menu.

28. Choose Pop-up Menu again from the Design menu.

29. Choose <create> and fill in the following information:

Name:	**REPORTS**
Description:	**This menu lets you print labels or a report.**
Message line prompt:	**Use the arrow keys to select one of the menu options.**

30. Press Ctrl - End.

31. Type the following menu choices, pressing Enter after each line:

Print Labels

Print Customer List

Your screen should look like Figure 3-29. Next, size the menu box.

32. Press Shift - F7, press ↑ six times, and press Enter.

33. Press F7 (Move) to move the box.

34. Choose Entire Frame.

35. Move the cursor to row 2, column 28 and press Enter.

36. Choose Save Current Menu from the Menu menu.

37. Choose Put Away Current Menu.

38. Choose Clear Work Surface from the Menu menu.

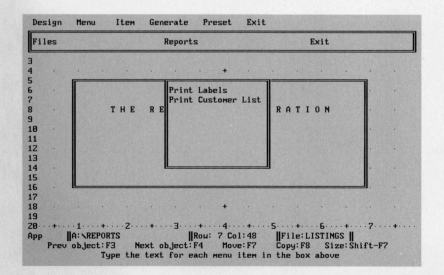

Figure 3-29

The Reports menu has only two commands: Print Labels and Print Customer List.

Now you are ready to attach the pop-up menus to the menu bar.

39.   Press [Alt]-D and choose Horizontal Bar Menu.

40.   Highlight MAINMENU and press [Enter].

The menu bar you created appears, with the cursor in it.

41.   Move the cursor to highlight Files.

42.   Choose Attach Pull-Down Menus from the Menu menu.

You are asked whether the pop-up menu should drop automatically.

43.   Choose No.

44.   Choose Change Action from the Item menu.

Another menu appears.

45.   Choose Open a Menu.

A form appears asking you to indicate which menu will be opened by this menu name.

46.   With the cursor in the Menu type box, press [Spacebar] until POP-UP appears.

47.   Move the cursor to the Menu Name box and type **files**

Your screen should look like Figure 3-30.

48.   Press [Ctrl]-[End].

49.   Press [Esc] to close the Item menu.

50.   Move the cursor to the next item on the menu bar, Reports.

51.   Repeat steps 42–49, typing **reports** instead of **files** for the menu name.

52.   Move the cursor to the Exit menu item.

53.   Choose Change Action from the Item menu.

54.   Choose Quit.

Figure 3-30

Here you designate what kind of menu will be opened by the menu named FILES.

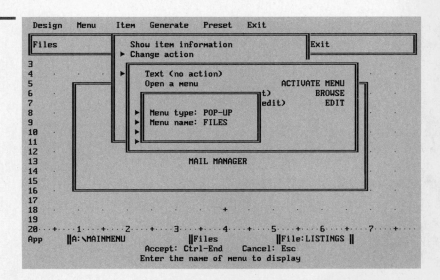

To save an application and keep working	Press [Alt]-A, S
To attach an action to an object	Press [Alt]-I, C
To generate code	Press [Alt]-G, set template to MENU.GEN, press B
To generate documentation	Press [Alt]-G, set template to DOCUMENT.GEN, press B
To save an application and exit	Press [Alt]-E, S

True-or-False Questions

Put a *T* next to each statement that is true. Put an *F* next to each statement that is false.

1. Working at the dot prompt is faster than working at the Control Center.

2. To start the Application Generator, type **create application** at the dot prompt.

3. Label forms are a lot like queries.

4. A relational database relates two or more data files so that you can use data based on the relationship.

5. The dot prompt command CREATE SCREEN MODULE creates a new data file.

6. The Application Generator lets you create professional-looking custom programs without being a programmer.

7. That two files are related means that they have a common field.

8. In a relational database, there must always be a controlling database and a controlled database.

9. When you create an application, the menus will not work if there is an object attached to them.

Multiple-Choice Questions

Select the best answer for each of the following questions.

1. Each database in a relational database is called
   a. a module
   b. a relative
   c. an entity
   d. a function

2. The part of the query design screen where you can type in links is the
   a. skeleton
   b. data panel

     c. Print menu

     d. none of the above

3. To test whether a link works, you use the

     a. test panel

     b. Edit screen

     c. Browse screen

     d. Create Link by Pointing command

4. The dot prompt command to run an application is

     a. DO

     b. RUN

     c. USE

     d. APPLY

5. To create a pop-up menu on the Application Generator work surface, choose

     a. Bar menu

     b. Pop-up menu

     c. Current menu

     d. Pull-down menu

6. What you type on the label form is

     a. printed at the top of each page

     b. repeated for the related field

     c. printed at the beginning of the report

     d. repeated on every label

7. The dBASE tool used to link relational data files is

     a. a report

     b. an application

     c. a query

     d. an entity

8. The first object the Application Generator asks you to create is

     a. the modules

     b. the welcome screen

     c. the bar menu

     d. the controlling entity

Review Questions

Briefly answer the following questions.

1. What are the four main steps in generating a custom application with the Application Generator?

2. Why is it better to relate two files with a customer number field rather than a customer name field?

3. How do you figure out which should be the controlling database and which should be controlled?

4. Why should you be careful when changing the structure of a database?

5. What do you take into consideration when designing a label?

6. What do you gain by using a relational database instead of using unrelated files to do the same job?

7. What is the importance of application documentation to a non-programmer?

Application Projects

1. Create a form-style quick-layout report based on the CUSRELAT query for the relational database you created in this lesson.

2. Run the DOMAIL application and print a set of labels.

3. Run the DOMAIL application and print a report.

4. Go to the DOS prompt and print the file DOMAIL.DOC. You can use the MS-DOS Editor or a word processor.

5. Run the DOMAIL application and add three records. (You make up the data.)

APPENDIX: dBASE IV COMMAND SUMMARY

At the DOS prompt:

To start dBASE	Type **dbase**, press `Enter`

At the Control Center:

To move the cursor to the menu bar	Press `F10`
To go to the Edit or Browse screen	Press `F2`
To go to the dot prompt	Press `Esc`, Y
To modify a database structure	Press `Shift`-`F2`
To open the Catalog menu	Press `Alt`-C
To use a different catalog	Press `Alt`-C, C
To create a new catalog	Press `Alt`-C, C, <create>
To add a file to a catalog	Press `Alt`-C, A
To print a Quick Report	Press `Shift`-`F9`
To open the Tools menu	Press `Alt`-T
To go to DOS Utilities screen	Press `Alt`-T, D
To quit dBASE	Press `Alt`-E, Q

At the dot prompt:

To use a data file	Type **USE** <filename>
To use an entry form	Type **SET FORM TO** <filename>
To enter data	Type **EDIT**
To go to the Control Center	Press `F2`
To go to the Control Center	Type **ASSIST**
To create a catalog	Type **SET CATALOG TO** <filename>
To change to a different catalog	Type **SET CATALOG TO** <filename>
To create a data file	Type **CREATE** <filename>
To create an entry form	Type **CREATE SCREEN** <filename>
To create a label form	Type **CREATE LABEL** <filename>
To create a report	Type **CREATE REPORT** <filename>
To create an application	Type **CREATE APPLICATION** <filename>
To make changes to an application	Type **MODIFY APPLICATION** <filename>
To modify a database structure	Type **MODIFY STRUCTURE**
To quit dBASE	Type **QUIT**

At the design screens:

To return to the Control Center	Press `Alt`-E, `Enter`
To move the cursor to the menu bar	Press `F10`
To see a pick list	Press `Shift`-`F1`
To sort a data file	Press `Alt`-O, S
To create an index	Press `Alt`-O, C
To create a Quick Layout	Press `Alt`-L, Q
To view a report on screen	Press `Alt`-P, V
To add a field	Press `F5`
To remove a field	Press `F5`
To save a report in progress	Press `Alt`-L, S
To create an extra line	Press `Enter`

To print a report	Press [Alt]-P, B
To save a report and exit	Press [Alt]-E, [Enter]
To begin/complete a selection	Press [F6]/[Enter]
To begin/complete a move	Press [F7]/[Enter]
To abort an operation	Press [Esc]
To open the Layout menu	Press [Alt]-L
To open the Organization menu	Press [Alt]-O

At the database design screen:

To return to the Control Center	Press [Alt]-E, [Enter]
To activate the menu bar	Press [F10]
To save a database under a new name	Press [Alt]-L, S, type <filename>, [Enter]
To insert a field into a structure	Press [Ctrl]-N
To delete a field from structure	Press [Ctrl]-U
To save changes and exit	Press [Alt]-E, S, [Enter], [Enter]

At the Edit or Browse screen:

To return to the Control Center	Press [Alt]-E, [Enter]
To move the cursor to the menu bar	Press [F10]
To go to the next column	Press [Tab] or [Enter]
To go to the previous column	Press [Shift]-[Tab]
To start a new record	Press [Pg Dn]
To go to the previous record	Press [↑]
To search for a record	Press [Alt]-G, F
To undo a change to a record	Press [Alt]-R, U
To toggle between Edit and Browse	Press [F2]
To mark a record for deletion	Press [Ctrl]-U
To unmark a record for deletion	Press [Ctrl]-U
To pack a data file	Press [Alt]-O, E
To create an index	Press [Alt]-O, C
To go to the query screen	Press [Shift]-[F2]
To save changes and exit	Press [Alt]-E, [Enter]

At the query design screen:

To return to the Control Center	Press [Alt]-E, [Enter]
To move cursor to the menu bar	Press [F10]
To add a file to a query	Press [Alt]-L, A
To create a link	Press [Alt]-L, C
To add a field to the view skeleton	Press [F5]
To remove a field from the view skeleton	Highlight the field, press [F5]
To move the cursor to the previous skeleton	Press [F3]
To move the cursor to the next skeleton	Press [F4]
To save a new query and keep working	Press [Alt]-L, S, type <filename>, press [Enter]
To save a query and keep working	Press [Alt]-L, S, [Enter]
To save a query and exit	Press [Alt]-E, [Enter]

At the Application Generator screen:

To move the cursor to the menu bar	Press [F1]
To place menu object on screen	Press [Alt]-D
To create a bar menu	Press [Alt]-D, H
To create a pop-up menu	Press [Alt]-D, P

To move an object	Press F7 , Enter , use arrow keys
To size an object	Press Shift - F7 , Enter , use arrow keys
To save the current menu	Press Alt -M, S
To remove a menu object from the screen	Press Alt -M, P
To save an application and keep working	Press Alt -A, S
To attach an action to an object	Press Alt -I, C
To generate code	Press Alt -G, set template to MENU.GEN, press B
To generate documentation	Press Alt -G, set template to DOCUMENT.GEN, press B
To save an application and exit	Press Alt -E, S

GLOSSARY

AND/OR condition: a condition that a user specifies in a query in order to search for a record meeting one and/or another criterion

application: a software program designed for a specific use

application definition screen: the screen where a user creates custom applications using the dBASE IV Application Generator

Application Generator: a dBASE IV feature that allows a user to create custom programs

ascending order: from a to z or 0 to 9; used for sorting and indexing

ASCII order: an order that recognizes uppercase letters as coming before lowercase letters; used for indexing

Browse screen: a screen that shows all the fields and records of a database arranged in columns and rows

calculated field: a field in a database report that calculates values based on expressions defined by a user

catalog: a group of associated data files, applications, labels, forms, reports, and queries

character field: a field set up to contain text, including numerals to be treated as text (such as an address)

code: elements of programming language that run dBASE IV

column layout: a layout that gives a line to each record

common field: a field that is the same in each of two or more data files, thus forming the basis for a relational database

concatenate: to chain together several parameters in an expression with a plus sign

condition: a value that is part of an expression; for example, *CA* in the expression *State* = "CA"

Control Center: the main screen where a user can use menus to carry out dBASE IV operations; more user friendly than the dot-prompt screen

controlling database: the data file that controls the other data files in a relational database; also called the *primary database*

custom data entry form: a data entry form designed by a user to meet his or her particular needs

custom report: a report designed by a user to meet his or her particular needs

database: (1) a set of information organized into records and fields; also called a *data file*; (2) a program that allows a user to enter, update, and retrieve data and to organize, search, and print that data

database design screen: the screen where a user defines the fields of a database, including name, type, and width

data file: *see* database

date field: an automatically formatted field containing the date

descending order: from z to a or 9 to 0; used for sorting and indexing

detail: the main part of a report, containing the fields

dialog box: a box in which dBASE IV asks a user to enter more information or to select from a variety of options

dictionary order: a sort order that recognizes uppercase letters and lowercase letters as the same

documentation: a printed list of the codes that have gone into a program created by the Application Generator

DOS utilities screen: a dBASE IV screen where a user carries out DOS operations such as creating directories and moving files

dot prompt: the dBASE IV command line where a user enters dBASE IV commands by typing the commands and pressing Enter; a fast, powerful alternative to using a Control Center

Edit screen: a screen that displays the fields of a database one record at a time; it is used for data entry and modification

entity: an individual data file in a relational database

entry form: a form for data entry; can be standard, as is the Edit screen, or custom designed

expression: a logical sequence of values, conditions, and operators used in sorting, indexing, and searching

field: a column containing like information about entries in a database

field name: a name used to identify the information contained in a field; limited to ten characters, including letters, numerals, and/or the underscore character

field type: the kind of field—usually character or numeric; *see also* character field, date field, logical field, memo field, numeric field

file skeleton: a list on a Query design screen that gives the name of the current database and each field of the database; the place where a user selects fields to create a query

fill-in box: a box that prompts a user to type in information

form layout: a layout that gives a line to each field of each record

forms design screen: the screen where a user creates a custom data entry form

index: a file that dBASE IV uses to arrange all records in ASCII order in a way defined by a user; does not change the natural order of records but gives a user a different view of them

key: *see* expression

label form: a form a user creates to print labels based on the fields of a data file

logical field: a field that accepts entries limited to Y (yes), N (no), T (true), or F (false)

memo field: a field set up to contain a note

menu: a list of commands

menu bar: a bar across the top of a screen that lists all the available menus

message line: a line at the bottom of the screen that suggests possible courses of action module: a file that forms a component of an application

navigation line: a line at the bottom of the screen that displays currently available commands

numeric field: a field set up to contain numerals to be used in calculations

operator: a symbol that expresses a relationship between the elements of an expression, such as = (equal to), (greater than), and (less than)

overwrite: to replace an existing file with another file having the same name

pack: to reduce a database in size by deleting marked records

page footer: information printed at the bottom of each page of a report, such as the page number

page header: information printed at the top of each page of a report, such as the title of the report, the date, and headings for each column

panel: a part of the Control Center that lists files within a catalog; this is where a user creates, modifies, opens, and closes files

pick list: a list of items from which to choose

picture function: a command that allows a user to choose formatting instructions for a report

pop-up menu: a menu of command options that appears when a user selects the command name on the menu bar

primary data base: *see* controlling database

QBE: *see* query by example

query: a question or series of questions that lets dBASE IV know what kind of data to retrieve

query by example (QBE):   a type of query in which a user enters search criteria into a file skeleton

query design screen: the screen where a user conducts a query

quick report: a report a user issues with a single command that gives the basics of a database as they are: all data arranged in rows and columns, names of fields at the tops of columns, and the date and page number on each page

record: a row containing all the information for a particular entry in a database

relational database: two or more data files that are related by a common field so that a user can find data based on all of them at once; eliminates duplication in data entry and saves disk space

report: information organized in a specific way; *see also* custom report, quick report

report design screen: the screen where a user creates a custom report

report intro: text appearing at the beginning of a report (for example, an explanation of what the report is about)

report summary: text or special fields appearing at the end of a report that calculate totals and averages of data in numeric fields

restriction: the part of an expression that specifies the field; for example, *State* in the expression *State* = "CA"

ruler: a bar on a screen that shows columns, tab stops, and margins and allows a user to change these settings

search: to look for something specific

sort: to physically rearrange records in a user-specified way, using dictionary order

status bar: a bar at the bottom of the screen that indicates the directory and pathname of the current file as well as the number of the current record and the total number of records in the file

structure: the way in which a database is organized; includes number, width, and type of fields

tag: the name a user gives to an index

template: a character string that allows a user to format data in a field; includes dollar signs, commas, and decimal points

view skeleton: a list on a Query design screen of the fields that will be used in the query

wild card: a character (such as an asterisk) that substitutes for any other character or characters

INDEX

Symbols

* wild-card character, 47, 73

A

Add Field window, 67-68, 69
    Calculated Fields panel, 68, 70
    formatting box, 67-68
    illustrated, 67
    Picture Function option, 68, 97
    Summary panel, 68
    Template option, 67, 97
AND/OR conditions, 74-75
Append/Edit Via Form File window, 110, 112
    illustrated, 111
application definition screen, 100, 102, 105, 111, 117
    definition form, 102
    illustrated, 101
    menu bar, 100, 101
    message bar, 100
    navigation line, 100
    status bar, 100
    welcome screen, 101, 102-103
Application Generator, 95-100
    for attaching actions to commands, 110-116
    commands, 120-121
    in designing menus, 103-110
    for documentation generation, 117
    function of, 95
    for generating code, 116-118
    starting, 100
    using, 100-103
    work surface, 101
applications, 95-103
    changing, 119
    creating, 95-100, 119
    generating code for, 116-118
    planning, 95
    procedure for creating, 95
    See also application definition screen; Application Generator
Applications menu, 102
    Display Sign-On Banner command, 103
    Save Current Application Definition command, 103, 110
Applications panel, 100
ASCII order, 58
AUTOEXEC.BAT file, 3

B

boxes, 33
Browse a Database file or View window, 113
    illustrated, 113
    options, 113-114
Browse screen, 23-27, 57, 62, 78, 94, 118

changing to, 26
commands, 39-40, 79-80, 120
Edit screen toggle, 80
entering data in, 38
going to, 39, 78
illustrated, 23, 26
menus, 24
moving within, 24
record display in, 35
saving changes from, 80
status bar, 24
See also Edit screen; Fields menu

C

catalog
    adding file to, 119
    bar, 21
    creating, 18, 118, 119
    defined, 4
    extension, 4, 18
    files, 4, 5
    files pick list, 88
    name, 4, 5
    using different, 118, 119
Catalog pop-up menu, 5
    Add File to Catalog command, 6
    closing, 7
    Edit Description of Catalog command, 6, 7
    Modify catalog name command, 5, 18
    opening, 39, 88, 118
    pick list, 5, 6
    Use a Different Catalog command, 88
Change Action menu, 112
    Browse command, 113
    Display or Print command, 114, 115
    Edit Form command, 112
    illustrated, 111
character fields, 10, 14
    quotation marks and, 59
    See also fields
commands
    Application Generator screen, 120-121
    attaching actions to, 110-116
    Control Center, 39, 78-79
    database design screen, 119-120
    design screen, 39-40, 79
    DOS, 39, 78
    Edit/Browse screen, 39-40, 79-80, 120
    query design screen, 119
    search, 47
    See also commands, dot prompt
commands, dot prompt, 16, 39, 79
    ASSIST, 79, 119
    CREATE, 16, 95, 97, 98, 119

CREATE APPLICATION, 100, 119
CREATE LABELS, 119
CREATE REPORT, 119
CREATE SCREEN, 16, 17, 97, 119
DISPLAY, 95
DO, 104
EDIT, 53, 79
F2, 39, 79
MODIFY APPLICATION, 105, 119
MODIFY STRUCTURE, 16
QUIT, 39, 79, 119
SET CATALOG TO, 119
SET FORM TO, 53, 79
USE, 16, 53, 79, 95, 98
Control Center, 4-15
    catalog name, 4
    commands, 39, 78-79
    going to, 39, 79, 119
    illustrated, 4
    menu bar, 4, 5-9
    message line, 4
    navigation line, 4
    Quick Report command, 25
    quitting from, 3
    screen, 5
    screen title, 4
    See also panels

D

data
    displaying, 23-27
    entering, 19-23, 119
    integrity, 20
    See also data files
database
    applications, 95-103
    defining, 17-19
    displaying, 12
    flexibility, 2
    link, 89-90
    pack, 50, 51-52, 53
    primary, 85
    relational, 84-89
    sorting, 54-58
    See also database structure
database design screen, 10, 16, 36, 56, 60, 86, 97
    commands, 39-40, 119-120
    Field Name, 13, 18, 86
    Field Type, 13-14, 18, 37
    illustrated, 13
    Index box, 37, 58
    Width box, 18, 37
    See also Layout menu; Organize menu
database structure
    categories, 1-2
    defining, 17-19